Advance Praise for *Catching the Light*

"A captivating memoir that showcases Harold's profound wisdom and sophistication as a photographer, filmmaker, and now as a writer. His storytelling is joyous and unpretentious, offering readers an inside look at his striking photography and dynamic films. It's a magic carpet ride through his life, making readers feel part of his journey."

—Al Pacino

"The actor/director relationship is an odd, yet amazing tango of inspiration, dedication, and, yes, manipulation. Harold's lovely, deeply personal prose gave me an insight that I never fully grasped until I was fortunate enough to read *Catching the Light*. To be privy to the artist's mind at work is a rare gift for the reader."

James Woods

"Harold is a dear friend and filmmaker I admire tremendously. I will forever be grateful for the opportunity of not only being in *TAPS* but for his generosity in allowing every door of the production to be opened for my edification. I studied every department, every aspect of this film production with his encouragement. It helped form the very foundation of my cinematic education."

—Tom Cruise

"Mr. Becker and his generation of artists gained their reputations by making films with realistic backbone. Courageous dramas that focused on the working class. Stories that addressed social injustices with characters that often questioned authority. How lucky we are to have been witness to such genius."

—Matthew Modine

"Harold Becker comes right at you, with the simplicity, directness, and challenge of his name. He's anonymous yet everywhere in his work, never calling attention to himself all the while turning a sire toward the agonizing pain and astounding beauty of life. A life lived in parallel observation and participation. Harold's sweet yet unexpressed desire for anonymity makes his work explode, an artist not only interested in cutting out what doesn't belong, but framing what does; the evidence revealing the subtext of a military school in *TAPS,* a corrupt municipality in *City Hall*, a romance giving birth to distorted lives in *Sea of Love,* and a police procedural that overcomes procedure with character in *The Onion Field*. Perhaps what makes Harold Becker is his shrug to anonymity, an unchallengeable pedigree of the Bronx and a tailor-father born in the nineteenth century, informing his intent to cut away everything, not only his photographs but his features, that isn't 'life.'"

—Bo Goldman,
Two-time Oscar-winning Screenwriter

CATCHING THE LIGHT
A MEMOIR FROM BEHIND THE LENS

HAROLD BECKER

PERMUTED
PRESS

A PERMUTED PRESS BOOK
ISBN: 979-8-89565-264-0
ISBN (eBook): 979-8-89565-265-7

Catching the Light:
A Memoir from Behind the Lens

Cover design by Garson Yu
Cover construction by Conroy Accord
Cover photograph by Harold Becker
Interior design and composition by Kate Harris

This book, as well as any other Permuted Press publications, may be purchased in bulk quantities at a special discounted rate. Contact orders@permutedpress.com for more information.

This is a work of nonfiction. All people, locations, events, and situations are portrayed to the best of the author's memory.

PERMUTED PRESS

Permuted Press
New York • Nashville
permutedpress.com

Published in the United States of America
1 2 3 4 5 6 7 8 9 10

For Susan

TABLE OF CONTENTS

CHAPTER 1
DRAWING CAME EASY

Herbie Sachs was my first best friend. We were four years old and lived in the same building, a five-story apartment house in The Bronx. Years later, I learned that The Bronx was the only borough that had a "the" in its name. I guess coming from The Bronx, that somehow distinguished it. In any case, the apartment house I lived in was one of thousands of similar buildings in The Bronx, which was pretty much a bedroom community. Row after row, block after block of dark-red brick, four- or five-story faceless buildings that lined the sidewalks, not a tree in sight, with the exception of the Grand Concourse, which was our Champs-Élysées. In fact, many of the buildings on the Grand Concourse were faced in a white brick, which distinguished them from their poorer neighbors.

Herbie lived on the third floor, while we lived on the first. My older sister was crippled with polio, and it was too difficult for her to climb stairs. Herbie and I spent most of our time playing in the street, but one day, I was in Herbie's apartment when his father, Mr. Sachs, a large heavyset man, was yelling at Herbie's older brother, who couldn't have been more than eight or nine years old. They were in the kitchen, and Mr. Sachs had Herbie's older brother backed up against the wall as he screamed at him and then slapped him again and again. It terrified me.

Mr. Sachs loomed large in my world. He was a high school teacher, and even at the age of four, I knew he was an important man. These were the darkest days of the Depression, and even I knew that having a steady job—being a teacher no less—gave Mr. Sachs a powerful presence.

I remember that when he sat down on the stoop in front of the building, he would first take out his handkerchief and brush the steps off before sitting down. I was told he did that to make sure there were no tacks on it. Of course it connected with his being a teacher. There probably were comics, of which I was an avid reader, that planted this idea in my head.

My father was a skilled lady's tailor. He told my sisters and me stories about growing up in a small shtetl near the Dniester River in what is now Ukraine, close to the western border of the Carpathian Mountains.

My father was a great storyteller. His favorite authors were the Yiddish writers Sholem Aleichem and Isaac Peretz. He would often read their works to us. But the stories I remember most are the ones he told me about his childhood. His family was poor; his father was a butcher, and his mother had died giving birth to him. He was raised by the oldest of his four sisters.

One day, a poor woman brought a chicken in to be slaughtered. My grandfather, thinking the chicken looked sick, sent my father, who was eight at the time, with the chicken to ask the Rabbi whether it was kosher. When the Rabbi refused to give it his blessing, my father, feeling sorry for the poor woman, told my grandfather that the Rabbi had declared the chicken kosher. For his "good deed," my father got a terrible beating. As he said, his father beat God out of him.

Unlike most immigrants, who bring over family members once they've established themselves in their new country, my father never asked his family to join him, as far as I know. Perhaps it's a reflection on how difficult his childhood had been.

When he was nine years old, he was apprenticed to a tailor in the next village some ten miles away. That night, he ran all the way home. Of course, he was returned to serve out his apprenticeship.

His family saved the pennies he had earned as an apprentice and bought him a ticket to America when he was fourteen. He made the journey alone, traveling across Europe to Hamburg, Germany, where he boarded a ship bound for New York. Yiddish and Russian were his native tongues. I remember him telling me that while boarding the boat in Hamburg, a woman who was sending her son to America unaccompanied asked my father to look after him. The boy was my father's age.

English was a foreign language to him, and he spoke it with an accent. Even though he served in the United States Cavalry during World War I, he never lost his heavy accent. He was not an American like Herbie's father, Mr. Sachs.

On Sundays, my dad would take me with him to buy a newspaper. The newsstand was in an underpass at the entrance to a subway station. One Sunday, Mr. Sachs was at the newsstand when we arrived. My father bought a copy of *The Freiheit*, a left-wing Yiddish newspaper that he always read, and suddenly there was an uproar. Mr. Sachs was yelling at my father, calling him a communist. My father answered back. He wasn't afraid of Mr. Sachs, but I was. I shrank in terror and shame.

It was the Depression, and while everyone in the neighborhood seemed to be in the same boat, there was clearly a top deck, and Mr. Sachs was up there. The die was cast; I was an outsider. But my father wasn't. He was outgoing. He could talk to anyone and did. He had traveled from the foothills of the Carpathian Mountains to New York alone. He spoke three languages, albeit with a heavy accent.

On Sundays, he often took my sisters and me on excursions downtown. Unlike Brooklyn, The Bronx didn't have a downtown. Downtown meant Manhattan. Sometimes, we took the subway all the way to Battery Park and then got on the ferry to Staten Island. We would pass the Statue of Liberty and ocean liners sailing toward port on our brief cruise. The subway opened the world to us.

The police stables near Central Park were a special attraction to me. My father had served in a cavalry division at Fort Ethan Allen in Vermont during World War I. His regiment was set to ship out for Europe when the war ended, so he never saw combat. This was brought home to me when veterans of the war were given bonuses, which were desperately needed in the depths of the Depression. We received six hundred dollars, enough to pay a year's rent for the basement apartment we were living in. Our next-door neighbor, the building's superintendent, received a two-thousand-dollar bonus, a fortune at the time, because he had seen action. I remember thinking how lucky he was.

Walking through the police stables, the horses towering over me as we passed them, my father would pick me up to pet them.

Horses were all I seemed to draw when I was a kid.

Drawing came easy to me. In elementary school, we would have class projects where the teacher would tack large sheets of drawing paper across the walls of the classroom and the class would "participate" in illustrating historical scenes from American history. Washington crossing the Delaware was a popular one. What class "participation" really meant was that two or three of the "class artists" would do the murals and thus avoid doing onerous school work. Being able to draw had its advantages.

My high school was an enormous red brick building at the end of the bus line. It was three stories high and a couple of blocks long. If they had put bars on the window, it would have passed for a penitentiary. Its inmates, four thousand boys, all being regimented to march in step. Any spark could set off the anarchy that lay just below the surface in every boy's heart. Word of an attractive young substitute teacher would fill the halls outside her classroom and bedlam would reign until order was restored.

Ms. Finch, my art teacher, was an oasis in the desert. Young and beautiful, she had blonde hair and long legs. She would sit on her desk in front of the room, her legs dangling, and I did everything I could to please her, bringing in drawings every day for her approval. They were usually done in charcoal, my subject the vistas seen from the roof of my apartment building. Our rooftops were our landscapes. I spent hours on that roof drawing my surroundings for Ms. Finch.

After high school, I was accepted at Pratt Institute, an arts school in Brooklyn, one hour away by subway. One long ride to the Hoyt Schermerhorn Station and then a local for the last two stops.

That became my routine for the next four years. Pratt was a world apart. I went from a school with a student body of four thousand boys drawn from the local neighborhoods to a school with about four hundred students from all over the country and was coed.

I had entered another world. I was in a foreign country. The fine arts program I had chosen had about thirty students in it, almost all of them girls. Most of them were from out of town and they were as exotic as my new surroundings. This was 1945, and we were still at war. That's where the boys were.

I tried to get transferred to one of the other programs the school offered. Illustration, industrial design—anything as long as it had more boys in it. I went to see the head of the school, Dean Boudreau. He had a waxed mustache that was twirled up at its ends. He was as foreign to me as the rest of the surroundings. Turning down my request, Dean Boudreau explained that I was on the boat to England; the boat to France had already sailed.

I quickly bonded with the one boy in my class. He was from Brooklyn. As my father would say, he was a "landsman," and he was way ahead of me as an artist. While I was drawing horses with four legs, he would often draw them with six legs or more. His trees had children hanging upside down from them.

It wasn't only the teachers, but my fellow students and the galleries and museums in Manhattan that opened the world to me. Pratt was really a vocational school. We were learning skills that would get us jobs in the real world.

Early on, Dean Boudreau addressed an assembly of first year students, welcoming us to the school. He spoke of what awaited us if we did well and then he paused. Looking around at the assembly, he informed us that only about 15 percent of us would ever find work in the field of art. I'm sure everyone in that hall thought they would be in that fifteen percent. In fact, our advisor, Mr. Robertson, informed us that there was no point in him trying to remember our names since most of us wouldn't be there in a year or two. By the end of the fourth year, of the original thirty, there were twelve students left in my class.

In my four years at Pratt, two teachers made an impression on me. One, Miss Tucker, taught painting. She was an older woman and always wore a wide-brim hat. This alone would have set her apart. I had done a painting of the street corner I used to hang out on with my friends. It was a night scene, the corner illuminated by the windows of the drug store that occupied that corner. It was raining, and a group of us were huddled under the drug store awning, silhouetted against the lit window.

In her weekly criticism, Miss Tucker singled out my painting for praise. I hadn't thought that much of it myself, it wasn't Edward Hopper.

Working in oils, I painted a portrait of my mother. She had a pensive downward stare. There was a darkness in her that reached out to me. While I was never satisfied with the likeness of my portrait, over the years my mother and my portrait of her slowly started to merge.

Miss Tucker also read palms and, after tracing my life line, told me I would live a long life. While I didn't end up pursuing a career in painting, I have lived a long life.

Another teacher who took an interest in me was Dr. Pritchard, my psychology teacher. Yes, we were required to take some academic subjects to qualify for a degree. Dr. Pritchard's real interest was in testing. I believe she was trying to develop an aptitude test to determine who belongs in an art school. Rorschach tests were very much in vogue then, and Dr. Pritchard gave me a series of Rorschach tests as part of her effort to develop an art aptitude test. Rorschach tests record a person's interpretation of a series of inkblots. Analyzing the results, she told me that I tended to see things in black and white, and this might be a problem for me later in life. I didn't think much of her prognosis at the time, but in retrospect, for better or worse, I've never been plagued with indecision. So maybe there is something in those inkblots.

Even though I had a partial scholarship, I still had to work part time. Art supplies were a major drain on my limited funds. The school was filling up with returning veterans, and under the GI Bill, they could buy all the arts supplies they needed. I looked on with envy.

I got a job working part-time in the display department at Arnold Constable, one of the luxury department stores that lined Fifth Avenue. The war was over and people were shopping. The department stores were thriving, their windows on Fifth Avenue a cornucopia of fashion.

The display department's major tasks were creating window displays that brought shoppers in. I remember designing a surreal train station out of slats of wood that was the background for the mannequins posing in their suburban clothes.

Every Wednesday night, we changed the windows. Each week brought a new display. For that one night, the store was ours—dressing the mannequins and installing the displays we had created the previous week. It was like Mardi Gras, music blasting and mannequins being danced down the aisle in the arms of window-dressers. Even the soda fountain—yes, the store had one—was ours. The display department was predominantly gay, and in the early morning hours, their friends outside would tap on the store windows to contact those working on the displays inside, arranging to meet after work. Bickfords on 42nd Street, a twenty-four-hour cafeteria, was their favorite rendezvous.

I was a provincial from The Bronx, and here was a world of fantasy and playacting. Each set of windows had a theme, whether to celebrate a holiday or the coming season. The mannequins were our cast.

From Bergdorf on Fifty-Ninth Street to Lord & Taylor on Thirty-Seventh Street, Fifth Avenue was a shopper's paradise. Now, most of them have been replaced by office buildings.

CHAPTER 2
FREELANCE

My real education started when I graduated from Pratt and had to get a job to support myself. I had a fine arts degree, which qualified me as an art teacher, so I got a job at an all-girls art high school teaching drawing. Fresh out of school, I was only a few years older than my students.

In my classes, the students would act as models for one another to draw. I often would read *The New York Times* while they were completing their drawings. It's a habit that was probably ingrained in me during the long subway rides to Pratt. Invariably, the school principal would stop by while I was reading. His timing was perfect. I knew my days were numbered.

Not that I would have stayed much longer. I wanted to be doing the work myself rather than teaching others.

I soon got a job with Courtland Displays, a design firm that created point of purchase displays, which were basically posters that advertised a product. They would be placed near the cash registers to tempt buyers, promoting everything from lipsticks to watchbands.

I was given a large drawing table and a taboret for my art supplies. My first assignment was designing a point of purchase poster for Speidel's expandable watchbands, which came in gold and silver. After I went home that night, I noticed my hands had turned purple. I washed and washed them, but I couldn't get the color off. I had been using paint that day, but none of it matched the purple on my hands.

The next day, the mystery was solved. It seemed that someone had been stealing the Speidel watchbands, and my boss had the brilliant idea of putting this invisible powder on the watchbands to catch the thief. Of course, it had misfired. I couldn't have been the thief; I had only been there for less than a week.

I was so incensed that they would go to such lengths to catch someone for lifting some cheap watchbands that I quit that day.

It was the last time I ever had a steady job. From then on, I was self-employed. A freelancer. *Freelance* had a special cachet to it.

You were on your own—no boss, no punching the clock—but it was pure fantasy. I had given up a real job with a check at the end of the week. All I had was my school portfolio and some posters and design work I had done for ad agencies while I was still at school.

Fortunately, I was able to pick up work designing book jackets. It wasn't a panacea. They paid very little for book jackets, but the tradeoff was that your name was credited on the jacket. The meager sum they paid included the artwork and the typography. Fortunately, I had unemployment insurance to help tide me over.

When applying for unemployment insurance, you had to meet with a job counselor who would try to help you find employment. I wasn't looking for a full-time job, but that was the deal.

I shared a loft on West Twenty-Second Street with Irwin Horowitz, a friend from school. It was sixty bucks a month split between us. Irwin was the "landsman" I had met in my first year at Pratt. We had much in common. We were both outsiders—he from Brooklyn, me from The Bronx—in a school that was filling up with veterans. It was 1945 and they were coming home. There was nothing romantic about this loft. It was in a rundown, rat-ridden building with few amenities, but it was a place to work. We complemented each other, so it felt natural for us to end up sharing a loft. We didn't know where we were going or where it would lead, so just a year out of school, we joined forces. We didn't even know how we could pay the rent, but we were young and stayed afloat on our ambitions and lunch at the automat around the corner on Twenty-Third Street. We were ready to take on anything that would pay the rent. Irwin did murals of kids hanging upside-down from trees on the walls of a children's clothing store in The Village. I built the cabinets to go with it. I even did a mural for a cafeteria on Forty-Second Street. It was an ambitious undertaking, but I was twenty-three and nothing seemed out of reach. Perhaps my ignorance was an asset. I couldn't paint directly on the wall of the cafeteria since it was open twenty-four hours a day, so I came up with a plan that would allow me to paint the mural in the loft.

Canvas came in six-feet wide rolls. I simply designed the mural in three panels, six feet by sixteen feet long. I painted each panel in the loft, and then I hired a wallpaper hanger to mount the mural.

The cafeteria is long gone, along with my mural. I remember visiting a lawyer in an attempt to get the final payment for my work. I had been given the first half before starting. Otherwise, I couldn't have afforded the materials. Getting the second half brought me to the lawyer. It was my introduction to the legal profession. Hanging on the wall behind his desk was a quote from Abraham Lincoln: "Time is the only thing a lawyer has to sell." I realized that if I ever did get paid, most of it would end up in my lawyer's pocket.

The loft was on the fourth floor of a walk-up. One day, there was a knock on the door. No one ever came up there—no reason why anyone would. The knocking continued until I finally opened the door.

There, standing before me was the job counselor from the unemployment office. She was a kindly middle-aged woman who took her job seriously. As far as I was concerned, too seriously. I was dumbstruck. How was I going to explain that I was doing freelance work while collecting unemployment insurance? Fortunately, before I could even try to explain, she told me that she was looking for work for unemployed artists.

I realized that she didn't recognize me, and the shock of seeing her had rendered me speechless, long enough to allow her to speak first. Maybe it was the dark hallway we were meeting in. Either way, it was a close call.

At Pratt, I had been introduced to the Bauhaus, a German art design movement from the 1920s. It was a pivotal influence on me. I was drawn to its modernist aesthetic—the clean lines, the lack of embellishment, the great architects and designers who had created it, like architect Walter Gropius, architect Ludwig Mies van der

Rohe, photographer and designer László Moholy-Nagy, painter Paul Klee, and others, all Bauhaus luminaries. But perhaps the greatest influence on me was the work of Kurt Schwitters, one of the pioneers in the art of collage.

Kurt Schwitters incorporated fragments of newsprint, bus tickets, labels, and all the discarded detritus of everyday life, combining them to make new connections.

I had begun to create collages while at Pratt. It was a perfect fit for the book jackets I was designing. I'd combine disparate elements—fragments of a printed page, a photo—into an assemblage that was its own entity. The collage I created for *The Beachcombers*, my first book jacket, was an assemblage of everything from sand, seashells, footprints, as well as the book's title.

Book jackets opened the door to magazines, and soon I was doing collages for *Esquire*, *Seventeen*, *Cosmopolitan*, and others. Lou Dorfsman was a very talented art director at CBS. I believe he was responsible for one of the great icons, the CBS Eye. Lou hired me to do a collage of the street signs of the small cities like Beverly Hills and Burbank that make up LA County. It was an early introduction to the Gold Coast.

Collages are, by their nature, three-dimensional. In order to prepare them for the printed page, they had to be photographed. I found a young photographer, Otto Maya, who would subtly light my collages, resulting in a photograph that retained the dimensional quality essential to a collage.

CHAPTER 3
PHOTOGRAPHY

Otto's studio was at 80 West Fortieth Street, across from Madison Square Park. It was a building filled with two-story studios. Irving Penn and Leslie Gill, among other photographers I admired, had studios there.

I got a call one day from Art Kane, the art director of *Seventeen* magazine. While I had received some recognition for the covers I had done, I was still living hand to mouth. Like the book jackets, they paid very little. The reward was that your work was credited. Art Kane introduced me to Jerry Plucer, a major fashion photographer who wanted to bring some young talent into his studio.

Plucer's studio at 235 East Thirty-Fifth Street was a carriage house. I remember entering through the driveway, passing Jerry's silver Cadillac Eldorado convertible—the height of luxury at the time—and entering a large two-story studio. I had entered another world.

Jerry Plucer had been a very successful fashion illustrator in Paris in the thirties. Carmel Snow, the editor of *Bazaar*, and Alexey Brodovitch, its art director, brought him to New York. He quickly realized that his future lay in fashion photography, and he was good at it. As he said, he could photograph in an hour or two what took him days to do as an illustrator. Photography had pretty much replaced illustrations in fashion magazines by then.

Plucer had a proposal for me. He had a smaller studio upstairs where I could do my collages, and more to the point, still lifes, sometimes called tabletop photography.

I knew little about the technical side of photography. I had taken a photography course at Pratt. It was mandatory, otherwise I probably wouldn't have taken it. My interest lay elsewhere. The school would lend us Rolleichords, two and a quarter by two and a quarter reflex cameras. Drawing influence from Moholy-Nagy, the great Bauhaus photographer, I would take pictures of fire escapes and the shadows they cast, sewer gratings, and other strong design elements. I'd never considered photography as a career, yet here I was, being offered just that.

In a strange way, turning to photography was an advantage. I had no mentor to shape what I did. I was learning as I went along. Plucer provided me with a very knowledgeable assistant who made up for my technical ignorance. My ignorance was an asset in a way. I learned by experimenting, trying things.

Lighting was my greatest challenge. I remembered being in Leslie Gill's studio. It was painted white, and he would simply bounce the light off the ceiling, creating a soft overall light. Irving Penn approached lighting in an altogether different manner. He used light that was strongly directional. I remember standing in the doorway of his studio, watching him work. I'm sure they thought I was a messenger making a delivery. I was learning from masters.

And, of course, there was Jerry Plucer, who, while not a mentor, was at the center of it. I was working completely independent of him and we had little in common, but I was witnessing it all. The high fashion models, the editors, the makeup and hair—it was a world of style and sophistication.

Plucer's light source was an enormous bank of reflector lights mounted on a frame set on rollers, easily ten feet by ten feet, that contained about thirty or forty reflector bulbs. The bulbs were diffused through sheets of tracing paper to create a source of soft light, acting as an artificial skylight. Years later, I saw the same principle employed in film studio lighting, sometimes called "Wendy Lights," which were invented by the great cinematographer David Watkin, whose nickname was "Wendy."

The studio was represented by a hard-charging agent, Al Wade. I always remember him wearing dark blue suits and brown shoes. It was a statement.

Wade introduced me to Hans Sauer, the art director behind an iconic ad campaign for Old Gold cigarettes. The ads were no more than a lit cigarette in an ash tray, beautiful smoke patterns rising against rich, dark backgrounds. Mr. Sauer thought I might bring a fresh look to the campaign. I did about a dozen sketches suggesting what I could do with these simple elements, the smoke patterns that were their signature. I remember Mr. Sauer sitting in his plush office, high up in a glass skyscraper on Park Avenue, my sketches all around him on the carpeted floor. He pointed his wing-tipped shoe at the ones he liked. He chose six. I was about to earn more for those six photographs than I had earned in the past year. It seemed simple. Find beautiful ash trays and backgrounds, and let the smoke patterns do the rest. I used a soft overhead bounce light, and the smoke rose beautifully against the dark backgrounds.

The only problem was that when photographed, the smoke was no longer there. It was frustrating. I could see the smoke curling up, filling the frame with its beautiful patterns, and yet when I photographed it, the smoke had disappeared. Again and again, I would change the lights and photograph my still life, rushing my eight-by-ten-inch negatives to the developer, always with the same result: The smoke had disappeared. I couldn't very well call on pros who had already done this. I was on my own. It took me three days and nights of experimenting with the lighting before I solved the problem. The solution was simple. As any professional photographer knew, you have to backlight smoke to see it on film.

I went from eating at Horn & Hardart, a chain of automats, to having a credit card and eating at any restaurant that would take it.

Automats had a novel approach to dispensing food. One wall of the automat was made up of small cubicles in which the food was displayed behind small glass doors with a coin slot next to each of them. By depositing a few nickels (nickels were the common denominator), the door would swing open and give you access to whatever was inside. For instance, a small jar of baked beans was two nickels. Another cubicle might have a bacon and egg sandwich behind the glass, which required four nickels. And so on. In the middle of the cafeteria was a glass booth where you would exchange your money for the nickels needed.

When I walked into Plucer's studio, I had entered a foreign world of fashion and sophistication. It was chic and rich.

The studio I worked in overlooked the large studio below, where Plucer did his work. The fashion models, stylists, hair dressers, makeup artists, and editors were all involved with helping Plucer create images for the pages of fashion magazines. The models were probably around my age, but they seemed older—on another planet. There was the iconic portrait he took of Lauren Bacall, then a fashion model, for *Harper's Bazaar*. Supposedly, director Howard Hawks, spellbound by the photo, cast her as Humphrey Bogart's costar in *To Have and Have Not*.

Jerry Plucer was an enigma to me. Our worlds were far apart. He was European and much older than me, his background cloaked in ambiguity. Though clearly talented, he played the chic card—down to the bespoke suits he wore while working. I remember being impressed that the buttons on his sleeves actually opened. To me, this was even more impressive than the El Dorado in the driveway.

Years later, I learned that his full name was Jerry Plucer-Sarna. In the back rooms of the studio, it had been bandied about that he had his roots in some Prussian nobility. As it turned out, his past was much stranger. His mother had been a concert pianist and his father an opera singer. They were Polish Jews and had perished in the Holocaust. His brother had been a hero of the Resistance. Jerry Plucer had created an entire persona. No wonder he was an enigma to me.

And then there were Jerry Plucer's friends, many of them European. New York was home to many of the emigrants that had fled Europe before World War II.

Among them, Eugen Schüfftan, a great Polish cinematographer, whose credits included some of the classics of German cinema, films like *Metropolis* (1927) and *Nosferatu* (1922). Despite Schüfftan's great international reputation, he couldn't find work here. The cinematographer's union, which was basically a father-and-son union, wouldn't accept him, and no film studio would employ him without a union card.

One day, Luise Rainer, the great film actress, came to the studio to be photographed by Schüfftan, an old friend. They had worked together in Europe. I remembered Rainer, I had seen her in *The Good Earth* in 1937, when I was about nine, at the Radio City Music Hall. I was overwhelmed by the opulence of the movie palace. I hardly remember the film, but what I remember most about the Music Hall was the men's room. The line of urinals were higher than me and seemed to go on forever. Louise Rainer won an Academy Award for her role in *The Good Earth* playing a Chinese peasant, and here she was being photographed by Schüfftan.

I watched in amazement as he lit her. He must have used at least ten lights, all narrowly focused. She seemed surrounded by lights.

It was so different from the lighting I had embraced: single source, simple, directional. When I saw the portrait Schüfftan had created, it looked like a movie still.

Schüfftan had taken an interest in what I was doing, and we would discuss lighting, of which he was, of course, a master. Even though he couldn't get work on films here, the film studios would hire him to light a difficult location. For example, he lit Carnegie Hall for a film of the same title, but of course, he wasn't credited. In discussing my work, he observed that while I lit for the printed page—the two-dimensional—in cinematography, one tried to create the illusion of depth—the third dimension.

Eugen Schüfftan finally got into the International Alliance of Theatrical Stage Employees (IATSE) through the back door. The National Association of Broadcast Employees and Technicians (NABET), an independent film union that he was a member of, was absorbed by IATSE. His first American film was *The Hustler* (1961), directed by Robert Rossen. Schüfftan won an Academy Award for it.

***

The interesting thing about freelance work was how varied it was. One day, I was challenged with photographing smoke patterns, another day, I was photographing a baby elephant standing on its hind legs, holding an Olivetti typewriter curled in its trunk.

It was Olivetti's idea of how to sell their new memory typewriter. Photographing it was another story. The Ringling Brothers Circus was in town, and I was able to hire their great animal trainer, Gunther Gebel-Williams. He was famous for training tigers to ride on the backs of elephants. He arrived at the studio with a baby elephant and an entourage of handlers following this "baby" into the studio. It hardly cleared the garage doors. Gunther explained that a baby elephant would be more trainable for the task at hand.

I noticed that Gunther's entourage carried a wheelbarrow, a shovel, and a large bag of carrots.

I had prepared the set and the lighting beforehand, knowing that any moving of lights or equipment might distract the elephant. Gunther had a very simple training technique: the carrot and the stick. When the elephant did what Gunther wanted, he got a carrot. When he didn't, Gunther struck him on the head with the stick. It was awful to watch; the poor animal would cry when he dropped the typewriter, knowing what was coming. But we did what we needed to do to get the shot. Well, we didn't do it—Gunther did.

In my expanding universe, I was commissioned by NBC to do a series of photographs announcing upcoming specials. It was the early days of television, long before the alternate universe of streaming changed everything. NBC was a leader in presenting some high-brow programming to go along with their more standard fare.

When I was a kid, there was Arturo Toscanini and the NBC Symphony Orchestra on the radio delivering programming that, with the advent of television, would become the foundation of PBS.

The series of ads I was commissioned to do included the opera *Madama Butterfly* with the great soprano Bidu Sayão. I crumpled up an enormous piece of white no-seam paper and surrounded her with it, her costume providing the only color. It was as close as I could get to advertising her upcoming performance.

Another photograph announced *The Stingiest Man in Town* (1956), a musical version of Dickens's *A Christmas Carol*, a perennial favorite, this one starring Basil Rathbone as Scrooge. Also featured was Martyn Green, the great Gilbert and Sullivan star of The D'Oyly Carte Opera Company playing Bob Cratchit. The photograph I planned was quite simple: in the foreground, an enormous close-up of the crotchety Scrooge; in the background, seated at a high desk, the timid Bob Cratchit.

In the short time I spent with the actors in costume and make-up, I realized that of course they saw themselves as stars, as equals, which they were, and here I was planning to photograph a glowering Basil Rathbone close-up in the foreground and Martyn Green seated on a high stool ten feet behind him.

I was so sure that Martyn Green would walk out that I spent most of the shoot directing him, trying to give him the feeling that the shoot revolved around him. An early lesson...

It was an eventful few years at Plucer's. It was my apprenticeship, even if I didn't realize it at the time.

There was an outpouring of creative photography in the '50s. I would look forward to the next issue of *Bazaar* with Richard Avedon's photographs of Dovima posing with elephants in Paris. He brought another dimension to fashion photography. He freed the models from their static poses. He caught them on the wing, in contrast to Irving Penn, whose powerful portraits in *Vogue* were of another order. W. Eugene Smith, Henri Cartier-Bresson, and other great photojournalists brought the world to us in the pages of *LIFE* magazine. These were my mentors.

CHAPTER 4
295 FIFTH AVENUE

My time at Plucer's was coming to an end. As was my relationship with my partner, Irwin. The artwork and collages we created lent themselves to close collaboration, but the move to Plucer's studio and my immersion in photography had changed that. I had become a photographer, and we went our separate ways.

But it wasn't as simple as all that. I needed a break and took off for the promised land: Europe. I had always dreamt of Europe. It was my lodestar—the cutting edge from which we all drew inspiration. The art and design of Bauhaus, the paintings of Picasso and Braque, the collages of Schwitters, the cinema of Fellini and Antonioni, and countless others that were changing the world I knew. At Plucer's, I had gotten a taste of that cosmopolitan world.

I landed in London with my Nikon S, a little jewel of a 35mm camera. Somehow, taking pictures made me feel at home wherever I went. It made me feel that I belonged. It took me to London, Paris, Rome, Athens, and points in between, all recorded on my Nikon.

***

Months later, I was home. I wanted my own studio and found it at 295 Fifth Avenue, a massive building that filled the block from Thirtieth to Thirty-First Street. Because of its high ceilings, it was filled with carpet showrooms. I found a great space on the seventeenth floor, perfect for a studio.

The seventeenth floor was set back and surrounded by terraces. Those on the north side of the building, where my studio was, overlooked the Empire State Building. The studio had beautiful north light but needed to have walls removed to open up the space.

The building manager directed me to the man who could do the job. He seemed to hold court on the loading dock. I had noticed him sitting there in the back of his limousine in his double-breasted suit. His limo seemed out of place among the trucks in the loading bay. Of course, he was running his cartage business from the back of that limo. He had mafioso written all over him. It was common knowledge that the mafia had a hand in the cartage business.

The key to demolition in a busy city is carting away the debris. That's where the man in the limo came in. His cartage company serviced the building. He gave me a price for the job, and in short order, the work was done.

When it was time to settle the bill, he informed me that the work had taken longer than expected, and he raised his price. I don't know what possessed me, but I said a deal's a deal and refused to pay more. He just stood there, the color rising in his face. He wasn't taller than me, but twice as wide. I realized that I had gone too far, but it was too late. He grabbed me and threw me up against the wall and held me there for what seemed like an eternity before dropping me and walking out of the studio. Clearly, he had gotten control of himself, probably remembering that he was now running a respectable business.

Years later, watching mafia movies, many of them iconic, I knew that they were fairytales. For a moment, I had come face to face with the real thing. I never forgot it.

***

295 Fifth became the center of my life. The long hours would start early, and I liked to have an hour or two for myself before the crew showed up. The assignments varied.

When I arrived on the scene, advertising was the lifeblood of the print world. Whether it was a fashion spread in *Vogue* or *Bazaar* or the editorial content of *The Daily News* or *The New York Times*, it was the advertising that paid the freight. The ad agencies lining Madison Avenue peddled the goods. Pages of beautiful models sold everything from clothes to cosmetics. The Friday night editions of newspapers were filled with ads for movies opening that weekend, in perfect symbiosis with the reviews, gossip columns, and background stories. It was an elite world I had entered. Photography told the story.

I remember a fashion spread I did for one of the fashion magazines: closeups of beautiful lips, a takeoff on Joan Crawford's "lips that won't quit", and the accompanying pages from Revlon advertising their lipstick.

Mademoiselle hired me to do a fashion spread of shoes and paired me with a young illustrator named Andy Warhol. Andy did beautiful drawings of the shoes, and I photographed the shoes against Andy's drawings. This was years before Andy did the Campbell's Soup cans. He was new to New York but had already established himself as a talented illustrator. We spent days working on the spreads, Andy telling me about his life growing up in Pittsburgh, doing illustrations for Kaufmann's department store (I knew of Edgar Kaufmann because he had commissioned Frank Lloyd Wright to design Fallingwater for him).

I was obsessed with lighting. How to create the magic that light brings to the subject, a portrait, a vase on a table—even a typewriter. I had been commissioned to photograph a new electric typewriter for the Royal Typewriter Company. I thought of a John Rawling photograph capturing a red convertible on a beach at sunset. Bathed in the soft diffused light of the setting sun—what we refer to as the magic hour and what the French would refer to as "*l'heure bleu*"—the car had a magical presence.

To create the same diffused light in the studio, I placed the typewriter on an elevated surface, and I positioned a strong light (my stand-in for the sun) beneath and behind the pedestal. I bounced the light off of a white tent that I had placed above the typewriter to simulate the sky. Just as in Rawling's photograph, the "sun" below the horizon had illuminated the "sky" above—I had created my own magic hour. John Rawling's car on the beach had become my Royal Typewriter.

Still photography became my métier, much as Jerry Plucer had envisioned for me. The commercial applications were limitless, whether photographing a typewriter or introducing the new Polaroid Land Camera. I photographed the back of the Polaroid camera with a hand peeling a fully realized photograph off of it. It became an iconic image.

I was hired to shoot a series of still lifes with the setting sun hovering like a bright orange ball in the background. I found a west-facing virgin beach in Puerto Rico, set up my still life, and waited for the moment the sun set to take the shot.

Unfortunately, the sun never diffused into the round orange ball I had envisioned. As a New Yorker, I had seen a thousand such sunsets to the west of the city. I realized that the sunset I was looking for was caused by the dust and smog that layered the city—not the clear light over a pristine beach.

All I got for my trip to that beach were flea bites. The "virgin beach" we had chosen included a stray dog. As I was crouched over my 8x10 view camera, a black drop cloth over me to block the sunlight off the back of the camera, the little dog joined me under the drop cloth. It was the only spot of shade on the beach, and he was sharing it with me. I was soon covered in flea bites, and the sunset I had come for was back in Manhattan.

I had gone from still lifes to baby elephants to creating a Mardis Gras parade for a car commercial in New Orleans. We literally took over Bourbon Street for two nights to create our own parade.

A series of portraits of athletes for *Sports Illustrated* brought in great athletes like Gordie Howe of the Detroit Red Wings and Y. A. Tittle of the New York Giants, both in the midst of championship seasons. *Sports Illustrated* had chosen well. Y.A. Tittle arrived at my studio surrounded by an entourage of admirers. My son, who was eight at the time, happened to be there. Y.A. Tittle, seeing him, pushed through the crowd of admirers around him and softly threw the football he'd been carrying to my son. That's class.

My studio was the nexus reflecting the work I was doing. On any given day, there might be Louis Armstrong with his effervescent personality, another day, Joe DiMaggio selling a coffee machine, or General Omar Bradley selling a wristwatch.

Omar Bradley was one of our very few five-star Generals. He had commanded the Allied forces in Western Europe during World War II. He arrived in beautifully-tailored civilian dress—as befit his new role as the chairman of the Bulova Watch Company—to be photographed holding aloft an Accutron watch, Bulova's first battery-driven watch.

It was a surreal experience. Here was one of our most famous World War II generals selling a wristwatch. My "directorial input" was asking him to hold the watch a little higher.

By an amazing coincidence, the house I am now living in was built by Omar Bradley in the early '60s—just around the time I was photographing him for the Bulova Watch Company. Serendipity, I've had my share of it.

Years later, meeting Ridley Scott in London, where he was starting his own production company called RSA, he reminded me that we had first met years earlier when he visited my Fifth Avenue studio when he had been on a traveling scholarship after graduating from the Royal College of Art.

While working for agencies and publications was all-consuming, I still tried to find time for personal work. I saw photographs everywhere: in a reflection in a store window, a couple in a bistro in a corner of their own, a lone man at a counter hunched over a cup of coffee. It was all there for the taking. All you needed was a camera and an eye.

CHAPTER 5
ELEVEN-BY-FOURTEEN

My 11x14 studio view camera

In the studio, I experimented with larger formats. I acquired a studio camera. It was enormous—the size of a guillotine. Despite its size, it was extremely mobile, and most importantly, it had long bellows and could take an eleven-by-fourteen-inch negative and produce an image of unmatched detail and tonal range. I did a series of portraits and nude studies; the eleven-by-fourteen contact prints they produced have a magic of their own.

The '50s and '60s were a world of change. Greenwich Village, where I lived, seemed to be an epicenter of that change. Around the corner was the Cedar Tavern, that storied bar where Jackson Pollock, Willem de Kooning, and countless other artists who were changing the art world hung out. By the time I arrived on the scene, they had mostly moved on to the Hamptons and points further west, but Cedar Tavern was still filled with their presence.

Max's Kansas City would later fill the void. I would run into Andy Warhol there, recording the scene with his Polaroid camera, as well as Allen Ginsberg, Arthur Miller, and other writers. It was a heady mix.

It was the '60s, but it had started a decade earlier, and cinema was at its cutting edge.

I had seen *Rome, Open City* (1945) when I was seventeen at the World Cinema on Broadway and Forty-Ninth Street. It was one of the only cinemas showing foreign films, an anomaly among the movie palaces that lined Broadway. *Rome, Open City* had a reality I had rarely experienced in films. No wonder—it was made right after the liberation of Rome. Roberto Rossellini, a great filmmaker, was equal to the moment. It ushered in a new movement in Italian cinema, referred to as neorealism, that portrayed the everyday life of post-war Italy. Its harsh realism was a revelation to me.

It was the beginning of my love affair with the foreign films that were pouring into the city. More art cinemas showing foreign films were popping up all over Manhattan in the '60s: the Bleecker Street Cinema, The New Yorker Theater, the Rugoff cinemas, the

Walter Reade Theater—all showing the films of Fellini, Antonioni, De Sica, the list goes on. An outpouring of talent. Film would never be the same.

Film seemed to be on everyone's mind. We'd all be talking about the latest releases. They were not simply entertainment. They challenged us and made for endless conversations.

The film that made the greatest impression on me was Michelangelo Antonioni's *L'Avventura* (1960). Its visual style, the images, the movement, the gestures, were allowed to play out and carry the story. The way that the subtext that spoke to the inner lives of the characters was new to me.

In a memorable sequence of wordless images, Antonioni reveals the underlying inner conflict that consumes his hero, Sandro. The setting for the scene was the square in front of the magnificent Palermo Cathedral. Architectural students are sketching the facade when Sandro enters the square, pausing before one of the sketches and deliberately knocking over the inkwell next to it, destroying the drawing. In that moment, Sandro reveals his inner turmoil. He once was one of these students, but is now at the beck and call of a real estate mogul.

I was drawn into a world so real, so intense and personal. The characters came alive—there was no artifice. They didn't feel like actors playing the part, they were the part. It was method acting before I'd ever heard of method acting.

I had grown up on Hollywood films. They were part of my childhood, but this era of cinema was different. It felt personal the way *Art* is personal. The way Marlon Brando broke through the fourth wall in *A Streetcar Named Desire*.

I had seen the play on Broadway in 1948 while still in art school. A group of us had gone to a matinee performance. It was a weekday afternoon, and the audience was mostly middle-aged women. We were behind them in the standing-room section. The theater was alive with their chatter as they shared boxes of chocolates. Then the lights dimmed, and the magic began. Brando was transcendent. Stanley Kowalski became a living presence.

One of the bars I frequented in the early '60s was the Limelight on South Seventh Avenue in the heart of the Village. What distinguished the Limelight was a small gallery off the main room. It couldn't have been more than twenty by twenty feet. Helen Gee, the owner, exhibited photographs in this small alcove. It was one of the few galleries exhibiting photographs at that time. Not many people collected or even thought of photographs as an art form then.

The Museum of Modern Art had a small photography gallery in the basement, adjacent to their screening rooms. It was there that I saw Robert Frank's *The Americans*. Fifty photographs, each of them a small masterpiece portraying life in this country in the '50s. A small sign announced that prints from the show could be purchased from the artist. Sixty dollars for an eleven by fourteen, ninety dollars for a fourteen by seventeen. That about summed up the value of photography in the early '60s. I bought a print. It was the beginning of my collecting, but I didn't know it then. I bought it more as a memento of my discovery of a great photographer.

CHAPTER 6
EUGÈNE ATGET
(1963)

I discovered Eugène Atget in the small gallery at the Limelight, and I fell in love with Atget's seven-by-nine-inch photographs capturing a Paris long gone.

From the turn of the century to the 1920s, he photographed Paris on his large view camera that accommodated seven-by-nine-inch glass plates. He took thousands of photographs of the city and its environs. In magnificent black and white, he captured the city's poetry, the early morning light coming off the Seine, the stillness of the boulevards, the floating gardens of Versailles, an organ grinder accompanied by a small child. You could almost hear her singing.

There is a stillness in Atget's Paris. Of course, the long exposure required at the time put anything in motion out of reach. In Atget's Paris, that stillness is a virtue. The world stops for a moment before moving on, forever preserved on a contact print from a seven-by-nine-inch negative.

The shadings from light to dark on those glass plates are no longer possible in modern photography. As our negative material and printing papers became more commercial, they set limits on the tonal ranges we could achieve.

A young American photographer, Berenice Abbott, an assistant to Man Ray at the time, recognized Atget's genius and befriended him. When he passed, it is our good fortune that he left her his life's work. Berenice, who became a major photographer in her own right (as I write this, she is having a major retrospective of her own work at The Met), devoted much of her life to bringing Atget's work to the world. Hence the exhibit of his photographs at Helen Gee's gallery.

I was so taken with Atget's photographs that I wanted to see more of them. By an amazing coincidence, it turned out that Joe Reynolds, my photography assistant, had worked as Berenice Abbott's assistant in the late '30s.

Joe introduced me to Berenice, and soon I was visiting her loft in the West Village. The walls were filled with shelves holding thousands of Atget's photographs. It was then that I thought of making a film, an homage to Atget. With Berenice's consent, I chose thirty-four images with the idea of creating a journey through Atget's Paris. I found a perfect accompaniment in the music of Erik Satie, a contemporary of Atget's. His *Trois Gymnopedies*, a twelve-minute suite, evoked the poetry of Atget's photographs. They set the mood, their tempo determining my moving into or out of each image as it dissolved into the next. It was a perfect marriage.

My film, simply titled *Atget*, was chosen for the first New York Film Festival in 1963. Seeing Atget's photographs on the big screen accompanied by Satie's score was a magical moment. The silver screen enhanced the beauty of the images. The dark theater—the only light and sound emanating from the screen—was hypnotic. It was a unique experience.

I had fallen in love with film and began to think about making other short films. It was such a natural progression from still photography. I had complete control of the work, I was able to finance it from my commercial photography projects, and the small crew I needed was already working with me.

The Bleecker Street Cinema had booked *Atget* to accompany its feature presentation *Children of Paradise* (1945), directed by Marcel Carné.

I was there the morning that it opened. There it was on the marquee: "Marcel Carne's *Children of Paradise*," and above it, "Harold Becker's *Atget*." To be sharing a marquee with the great French director Marcel Carné was overwhelming. But truly, it was Eugene Atget, another major French artist, sharing that marquee.

I met the distributor of my short film, Leo Dratfield, in the lobby. He was with the theater programmer who had booked our film to accompany the feature presentation. With cinemas showing foreign films all over the city, shorts were often included. Rather than have a blank screen between showings, short films would fill out the program. While discussing other short films Leo was representing, the programmer referred to them as "seat changers." I was taken aback, but, of course, that's what they were. Their function was to fill the time between each showing of the main feature. It may have brought me down to earth a bit. Still, the image of that marquee stayed with me.

CHAPTER 7

BLIND GARY DAVIS (1964)

In the early '60s, folk music was finding a wider audience. Woody Guthrie, Pete Seeger, and others of the immortals lead the way. Its apotheosis was Bob Dylan.

Woody Guthrie had been Dylan's mentor. I had seen Woody perform when I was sixteen or seventeen at a small club in the Bronx in 1944. He was already a legend in the folk world. We were in the middle of the war, and Woody had painted "THIS MACHINE KILLS FASCISTS" on his guitar.

My first live-action short was *Blind Gary Davis*. Reverend Gary Davis, a blues and gospel singer, was a powerful presence in the New York folk music scene. His rendition of "Death Don't Have No Mercy" was a haunting homage to his mother. After meeting the Reverend in his small apartment in Harlem, I was so impressed with the force of his personality that I knew I had the makings of a short. I would film him in his home and move out into the streets of Harlem as he sang.

I rented two Mitchell sound cameras because I was covering the Reverend singing, and I needed to be able to cut between two cameras that were in sync. I was learning...

The transition from photography to cinematography was simple; the principles were the same. After all, motion pictures basically were twenty-four still photographs per second running through a projector to create the illusion of movement. However, the cameras were very different. That part was new to me.

In still work, I owned all my own equipment, but for cinematography, I had to rent two 35mm Mitchells—large heavy cameras that hadn't changed much since the early days of cinema. We learned to load the cameras using the *American Cinematographer Manual*. I was learning by doing.

Even obtaining 35mm motion picture film was different. Unlike ordering from my local dealer, like I did for all my photographic supplies, I found that there was only one source for Kodak 35mm negative film. Whether you were an independent ordering twenty thousand feet of film or a studio ordering millions, the only supplier was the Hoffman Company in New Jersey and you had to pay up front. George Eastman, the founder of Eastman Kodak, had made a deal with Hoffman in the earlier days and remained Kodak's sole distributor. We had to send a messenger to Hoffman, cash in hand, to get the film. A new world to me.

Once we had our film, we loaded up our Volkswagen Bus and were on our way to Harlem. Days earlier, I had watched as a Hollywood crew set up lights for a night shoot on 5th Avenue. There were lighting and equipment trucks lining the avenue. I looked on in amazement. The logistics alone were overwhelming.

In my naivete, I felt superior to this. We loaded everything we needed plus a four-man crew into our Volkswagen Bus. Of course, we were shooting one man in a small room. As to filming on the streets of Harlem, our minibus served as a moving dolly. We simply slid the door of our van open and had a platform to shoot from.

Once we arrived at Gary Davis's home in a Harlem tenement, we dragged our heavy cameras and lights up flights of stairs to the Reverend's small apartment. The room we were shooting in was hardly big enough for the Reverend and our crew of four, not to mention the two large Mitchells. I had the Reverend sit in his favorite chair in one corner, a window opening onto a shaftway behind him, his large form silhouetted against the window.

I placed the two cameras, one at a wide angle that included Gary Davis and as much of his surroundings as we could frame in that small room. The other camera was focused on the Reverend. I had spent the previous week practicing with the wheels of the gear head so I could smoothly pan and tilt the camera, moving from a close-up on the Reverend's face to his hands playing the guitar.

The Reverend Gary Davis did the rest, telling us the story of his life, spelling it out on his guitar. He could literally make that guitar talk. He spoke of his mother, of how his first instrument was the washboard, and the first guitar his mother bought him.

He then launched into "Death Don't Have No Mercy."

"Well now death don't have no mercy in this land

He'll come to your house and he won't stay long
Look 'round the room and your mama will be gone

Death don't have no mercy in this land"

I overlayed the ballad with a montage of images of the people of Harlem in doorways, in the streets, standing on corners. My first live action film was fifteen minutes long.

It garnered its share of awards, handsome "diplomas" that acknowledged the fact that there was an audience out there, albeit a small one.

***

Film had become more of a presence in my life. I became a member of Cinema 16, where I saw the work of avant-garde filmmakers like Jonas Mekas and Hans Richter. Richter's film *Dreams That Money Can Buy* (1947) was emblematic of the work being done by independent filmmakers. The work was personal, and it found an audience in those weekly screenings on Sixteenth Street. It had nothing to do with commercial cinema. It was another world, a personal one.

My involvement with film took another surprising turn. TV commercials were knocking on the door. It was a natural transition from still photography ads to TV commercials. It was a tsunami. Suddenly television was everywhere, and with it came the ubiquitous commercials that paid the way. One day, I was shooting stills; the next, I was filming TV commercials for the same clients. It was the early days of sixty-second commercials, the chance to tell a story—albeit a very short story.

A beer commercial might start with an early morning vista of a water truck washing down the street, panning to shutters being pulled up to reveal a bar preparing for the day—a love letter to a Midtown saloon—and ending with a close-up of the beer.

It gave us the chance to make mini-movies and learn our trade. By then, I had what was for me, a larger crew. The intimacy of a still photography studio gave way to a small production company with a line producer and editor. In the early days, we produced the commercials from preproduction to the final release print.

Therein lay the rub: we were constantly on the clock. Time had become a major factor. From the shoot to postproduction, the release date dictated the schedule. I actually bought a stopwatch, as the sixty-second commercials we started with soon morphed into thirty seconds. Time was a strict taskmaster, but it did focus the mind.

CHAPTER 8
IVANHOE DONALDSON
(1964)

In the '60s, new wave French films like Jean-Luc Godard's *Breathless* (1960) and François Truffaut's *Jules and Jim* (1962) brought a new dimension to cinema. *Breathless* used "cinéma vérité," a new style of filmmaking that gave it a documentary feel. In America, the Maysles Brothers and D. A. Pennebaker were making documentaries, shooting on 16mm sound cameras that were light enough to be handheld and gave their films the mobility to connect with the subject more intimately, the very definition of cinéma vérité." Pennebaker's memorable documentary, *Don't Look Back* (1967), about Bob Dylan's 1965 tour of England was a perfect example of it.

Cinéma vérité was a perfect fit for my next film.

It was 1963. John F. Kennedy was president, and the world was changing. The Civil Rights Movement, led by leaders like Martin Luther King Jr, had gathered momentum in the early '60s. Voter registration, especially in the deep South, had long been suppressed. The student movement known as Student Nonviolent Coordinating Committee (SNCC), which was leading the voter registration drive in the South, had caught my attention. Ivanhoe Donaldson, a student at the University of Michigan, was heading south to help voters register in Alabama and Mississippi. I decided to document his journey. With an Auricon 16mm sound camera on my shoulder, I joined him as he went South. Our film would be a record of that journey.

Our first stop was Danville, Virginia. While we were there, we heard about the bombing of a Black church in Birmingham, Alabama, in which four young Black girls were killed.

I was in the middle of things, able to document the response by the Black community in Danville to this travesty.

I got my first taste of what lay ahead when I filmed in a Black church in Danville. Ivanhoe and other SNCC leaders were teaching young people how to protect themselves from possible police beatings before a sit-in at the Danville Courthouse the next morning to protest the Birmingham bombings. I was also there to film the sit-in and capture the bravery of these young people. Times were a changing, and this was just the beginning.

From Danville, we headed deeper south, through Georgia to Selma, Alabama. It soon became too dangerous for Blacks and Whites to travel in the same car.

By the time we got to Selma, I knew we were in a police state. The first thing we saw as we drove in was the radio tower that stood astride the Selma police headquarters. It was by far the tallest structure in Selma, part of a police presence that dominated the landscape. Eighty percent of the population was Black, but the power structure was White. Voter suppression helped explain why tensions were so high.

Only the presence of the FBI and the national press coverage made it relatively safe for us to film in Selma.

In order to register to vote, the Black citizens had to run a gauntlet of police from every jurisdiction in the state. City police, county police, sheriff's deputies, state police—even George Wallace, the governor, had his own police force. All in different uniforms, but all with the common purpose of suppressing the Black vote.

We filmed in a Black church where the air was filled with tension, and I was thankful that film crews from the national networks were there as well. The messianic preacher was telling his congregation a story about a bear walking through the woods. Winter was coming, and the bear was hurrying to the other side of the river where it was still warm.

As he gets to the edge of the river, he hears a plaintive voice calling, "Mr. Bear, Mr. Bear."

He looks down and sees a snake, half-frozen, covered in snow. The snake begs him to take him across, pleading "Mr. Bear, if I remain here, I will freeze to death."

The bear replies, "But Mr. Snake, if I pick you up, you will bite me."

The snake assures him, "Mr. Bear, if you save my life, I will be your friend forever."

Mr. Bear, touched by the snake's plight, picks him up, cradles him in his arms, and crosses the river. As they get to the other side, the snake, in the warmth of the bear's arms, comes to life, rears back, and bites him.

The bear cries out, "But Mr. Snake, you said that if I took you across, you would be my friend forever."

"Yes Mr. Bear, but you knew I was a snake."

The preacher was warning his congregation that despite the presence of white supporters coming south, they couldn't let their guard down.

The next stop was Greenville, Mississippi, a town in the heart of the Mississippi Delta. Fields of cotton bordered the river. The flat landscape and low horizon had its own magic, but it was the same story: an overwhelming Black population ruled by a White minority. Voter suppression was a way of life, and they intended to keep it that way by any means necessary, including murder.

Years later, Alan Parker's *Mississippi Burning* (1988) documented the killing of three civil rights workers just down the road from where we'd been filming in 1963. I slept with our return tickets under my pillow. My crew was ready to take the next flight out. Again, a federal presence was our umbrella, but what really sustained us was the courage of the SNCC kids and their supporters. It was also the first time I had heard of a white folk singer who went South to lend his voice. His name was Bob Dylan.

We were witnesses to history. Today, Greenville, Mississippi, has a black mayor.

Ivanhoe Donaldson premiered at the 1964 Mannheim International Film Festival. The Rubinstein Library at Duke University became its home.

CHAPTER 9
BRUCE GORDON (1964)

I met Bruce Gordon at the SNCC offices in Selma, Alabama. Bruce, like Ivanhoe Donaldson, had traveled to Selma to help get Black citizens registered to vote. I was caught up by his passion and intensity. I knew I had to try to capture that moment, so I decided to interview Gordon.

The SNCC offices were on the upper floor of an undertaker's parlor, open coffins on display on its porch, and it was across the street from the police headquarters, the largest building in town except for the courthouse. That alone tells you everything about the state of affairs in Alabama. It also speaks to the courage of the young people who had ventured south to help register Black voters. It was the reason my interview with Bruce Gordon was so compelling.

The seventeen uninterrupted minutes that I was able to film were made possible by the 16mm Auricon camera on my shoulder. It was true cinéma vérité. The interview was so powerful in its own right that I turned it into a short film, *An Interview with Bruce Gordon*, which ended up premiering at the 1964 Lincoln Center Film Festival as well as the London Film Festival. Being featured at film festivals was rewarding, as it was one of the few venues where short films could be seen.

CHAPTER 10
SIGHET, SIGHET (1967)

"Somewhere in Transylvania, in the shadow of the Carpathians, very near the most capricious frontier of Eastern Europe, once upon a time there was a dusty little town called Sighet. It is a town like many others, and yet it is not like any other. Quiet, withdrawn, resigned, it seems almost petrified in its own forgetfulness; and in the shame that springs from that forgetfulness....

"This was my town once; it is not my town now."[1]

And so begins Elie Wiesel's harrowing story, "The Last Return," which inspired my short film, *Sighet, Sighet*.

In 1944, at the age of fourteen, Wiesel and the other ten thousand Jews of Sighet, a small Romanian town on the Russian border, were loaded into cattle cars and deported to Auschwitz. As the only member of his family to survive the Holocaust, Wiesel returned some twenty years later to the town he had been deported from. Only now, there were no Jews. The main street of the Jewish section of the town, once thriving and bustling with commerce, was shuttered and silent. It is now called "The Street of The Deported."

I read Elie Wiesel's haunting story in *Commentary* magazine and knew there was a film there—a film I wanted to make.

I knew that in some ways, it was beyond me—beyond anyone who hadn't experienced the Holocaust firsthand—but perhaps I could tell it through Elie Wiesel's words. It was the power of his words that I became obsessed with. I recorded Elie Wiesel reading his story, and I was struck by how his voice evoked the horror of what he had lived through.

I traveled from New York to Sighet with Elie Wiesel, a journey that he was reluctant to undertake yet again. After just a day in Sighet, he told me he could not continue; it was too much for him. I stayed to photograph the town. My only guide was the one Jewish family living in Sighet that Elie had introduced me to. The

1 Elie Wiesel, "The Last Return," *Commentary*, March 1965, accessed online March 30, 2025, https://www.commentary.org/articles/elie-wiesel/the-last-return/.

language we had in common was Yiddish, and my command of it was very limited.

I never got to ask them why they had returned to a city of ghosts. Perhaps they were there to preserve what remained of the Jewish cemetery, which I visited with them. They also took me to see Elie Wiesel's former home, now occupied by others who had simply erased any trace of the family that had once lived there. They hadn't even bothered to remove Wiesel's family photographs from their frames. They simply placed their own pictures over them.

I photographed the synagogue, now a silent witness to a time when the Jewish inhabitants of Sighet couldn't even imagine what would befall them.

Early one morning, I was photographing at the railroad station where in 1944, the cattle cars had departed from Sighet to Auschwitz with the entire town's Jewish population of ten thousand men, women, and children. The railroad station is close to the Russian border, and I remembered Elie telling me that they could hear the sound of the advancing Russian armies in the distance as they were herded into the cars.

As I stood there on that station platform, imagining what had happened on that fateful day, I thought about how Yampola, the town my father came from, was just on the other side of the mountains I was looking at.

Suddenly, something poked me in the back. I turned to find a policeman with a rifle pointed at me. He barked commands, which I did not understand, and then, gesturing with his rifle, marched me to the police station. After showing them my passport, I expected an apology. Instead, they placed me in a very small cell. Being an American, I was sure they would quickly see the errors of their ways and release me. As the hours passed, I thought about how Elie insisted we register our journey to Sighet with the US Embassy in Bucharest. I thought it was needless, just paranoia on his part. I was thankful that we'd listened to him. It was the end of a very long day when I was finally released. It was a harsh brush with reality—I was in a totalitarian state and the ground under me was not as firm as I'd thought it was.

I met with Romania's Minister of the Interior about my plans to do a film about Sighet as I would need their permission to shoot there. Romania was a Communist state under Soviet influence at the time. I complained to the minister about being imprisoned for a day, and he laughed, explaining that he had been imprisoned by the previous regime for over ten years for being a communist. He told me, "A little prison time is good for a man." I didn't share his enthusiasm.

In any case, I was not granted permission to film in Sighet. I should have told them that I wanted to do a musical. I had to give up my idea of making a feature film in Sighet, but Elie's story still haunted me.

The sound of his voice carried all that he had lived through. That was the key. Jimmy Guiffre, the great jazz saxophonist, was my friend. I played Elie's narration for him, and he improvised on top of it. I underscored Elie's narration with Jimmy's haunting saxophone solo and combined the audio with the photographs I had taken in Sighet as well as vintage photographs that were the only record of Sighet's former inhabitants.

Sighet, Sighet was thirty minutes long, the length of Elie's narration. Too short for theatrical release, it found an audience at film festivals, schools, and other venues. It received its share of awards, but the one that stood out was the Gold Prize at The Mannheim -Heidelberg International Film Festival. It was literally a gold prize worth approximately five thousand dollars. It doesn't sound like much, but it was unusual to receive a financial award for a short. Film festival awards were usually beautiful diplomas that you could hang on your wall; financial rewards were almost unheard of.

Sighet, Sighet found a permanent home at Brandeis University, where one can access it. Of course, with the advent of the internet, I was able to put it on Vimeo.

All my thoughts now were on making a feature-length film. Everything I had done, wittingly or unwittingly, had led me to this. Getting through the door was another matter.

Most aspiring cinematographers went west to the mecca that was Hollywood. I was not interested in going to Hollywood, not that they were waiting for me. Hollywood, in spite of the brilliance of its moviemaking, seemed unapproachable to me. It was a behemoth. The studios were beyond me. I wouldn't know where to begin. I wanted to make my own films, just as I had made my own shorts.

European films had always been my primary source of inspiration, even though I had been brought up on Hollywood movies and looked up to directors like John Ford and other greats. My love affair was with the foreign films that were flooding New York. This is what I aspired to. The new wave of Italian, French, and now English cinema had opened my eyes to what was possible.

I was now spending more time in London. It was the '60s and like New York in the '50s, London in the '60s was the epicenter of the arts—music, theater, and film fueled by an irresistible surge of creativity. It was young and alive.

The world of UK commercials welcomed me with open arms. The British were just catching up with and surpassing what we had been doing in New York. But I viewed commercials in the rearview mirror.

I was looking for a story to tell, just as I had with my shorts, but now it would be a feature-length film. That was my Holy Grail. I had friends and contemporaries in the same boat, looking for a path to the promised land. My path was to find a story and take it from there. I had the means to take that first step thanks to my commercial work. I knew that if I could find a script I was passionate about, the rest would follow.

CHAPTER 11
THE RAGMAN'S DAUGHTER (1972)

I found what I was looking for in "The Ragman's Daughter," a short story by Alan Sillitoe about a love affair between Tony, a working-class boy, and Doris, the privileged daughter of a wealthy rag merchant. In England, a ragman had a different connotation than it did in the US.

In England, the rag trade might make you wealthy, but the stigma of it kept you an outsider, and Doris, though privileged, is an outsider. In rebelling against the hypocrisy of a class system that looked down on her, she found a natural ally in Tony, who was also in rebellion against a world that defined him. Together, they lead a life of crime, stealing from the rich and giving to the poor, thinking of themselves as modern-day Robin Hoods. Of course, a day of reckoning comes and reality grabs them by the throat.

Who better to write the script than the author himself? Alan had written screenplays for two of his books: *The Loneliness of the Long-Distance Runner* and *Saturday Night and Sunday Morning*, which had been made into memorable films by Tony Richardson and Karel Reisz (respectively). Both had made deep impressions on me.

Alan invited me to spend a weekend with him at his home in Sussex to talk about the script. It was a three-hour drive from London. As I drove south, the further I got from London, the more estranged I felt. What was I doing so far from home? Of course, I was at home in London—with the cosmopolitan atmosphere and big city energy, I easily fit in coming from New York.

Spending a few days with Alan dispelled all that. We had a lot in common, and I deeply related to the story he had written. It was about characters I identified with.

What draws you to a story—what makes you want to give it another life, to make a film of it? It was a story I could relate to. It was Alan's description of Doris, the ragman's daughter, riding a horse down a cobblestone street in a working-class neighborhood in Nottingham to visit her boyfriend, Tony. That was a visual image that only film could fully convey.

Within months, Alan delivered a script that fulfilled the promise of his short story. It was the older Tony looking back to that brief moment when he had fallen in love with the ragman's daughter.

Together with Souter Harris, who I had worked with in commercials and had a small production company, as my producer, and Michael Seresin, a brilliant young cinematographer who I had also worked with in commercials, I set sail. We were all neophytes and, more importantly, good friends with shared goals. We had a script we believed in and forged ahead.

Our $500,000 budget was minuscule even by independent film standards, but it was all I could raise. It seemed like I was constantly piecing the financing together only to see it fall apart again and again. I ended up financing much of the film out of my own pocket, the same way I'd financed my shorts. Shooting those hundreds of commercials bought me a chance to dream, to take another road and find out where it would lead.

It was my good fortune to have Miriam Brickman, a legend in British theater and cinema, as my casting director. Miriam was the casting director for the Royal Court Theatre and supervised casting for countless filmmakers such as Lindsay Anderson, Tony Richardson, John Ford, Woody Allen, and the list goes on.

She had worked with John Ford in Ireland on *Young Cassidy* (1965), one of his last films. It was a dark experience for Ford, and the credits reflect it. The film is credited to "Jack Cardiff plus one," the "one" being the legendary John Ford. Miriam was witness to the "suits" standing behind Ford on the set with their stopwatches.

Miriam's casting office on the fifth floor of a narrow building on Half Moon Street in SoHo was a sort of pilgrimage. It had witnessed the royalty of British theater and cinema climbing that narrow staircase. Miriam brought in a beautiful young actress named Victoria Tennant to play the ragman's daughter. She was everything I had envisioned for the role.

She was born into theater royalty. Her mother had been a Russian ballerina, and her father, Cecil Tennant, was an agent who represented Laurence Olivier and Ralph Richardson, who was also her godfather.

Simon Rouse, my other young lead, was equally talented but cut from a different cloth. He was from Bradford, a working-class city in the north of England. In a way, their contrasting backgrounds reflected the disparity of the characters in our film.

I had a good cast, and if I measured up, I would have a film that was the sum of its parts and hopefully more. There is an unknown chemistry in bringing together the cast, the cinematographer, the production designer, the costume designer, and all the other artists that bring a film to life. One moment, we are strangers; the next, we are intimately involved, giving ourselves over to telling our story.

I remember spending the first day of shooting at the side of my cinematographer, Michael Seresin, working on the lighting with him. Perhaps it was because I was most secure with this aspect of filmmaking, but after seeing that first day of rushes, I understood that I should leave the lighting to Michael, who was a master at it, and spend my time rehearsing with my actors.

It was a thirty-day shoot. Not nearly enough time, but it was all we could afford. We tried to make up for it by shooting long hours. Twelve-hour days became the norm. Somehow it was cheaper to go into overtime than to add days to the schedule.

It was not without its consequences. One night, Michael and I were working out a tracking shot that would take my two young actors through a railroad underpass. We were so concentrated on working out the task at hand that we lost track of time. We suddenly became aware that it was past midnight, and we were alone on the street in the middle of the night. The crew, who we'd assumed was waiting down the street, had disappeared. I was shocked to learn that they had called a strike and gone home. They'd had enough of the long hours. I felt betrayed. My relationship with the crew had always felt personal to me. From the time I had been a photographer, I identified with the people I worked with. We were in this together. If three people were lifting a table, I was there lifting the fourth corner.

It was a rude awakening—a cold dose of reality. I realized that for most of the crew, it was a job. For the few of us at the core of it, it was a calling.

It seems that the British film unions, which were all-powerful at the time, had rules that made it possible for even a minority of the crew to call a walkout. Their rules also made it impossible for me to fire anyone except for "personal reasons." I confronted each of them individually. It was an onerous task, but I couldn't work with people I no longer had confidence in. We became more sensitive to cutting back on the long hours, but my relationship with crews was never the same after that. Of course, my respect for the people behind the camera is unlimited; I feel I am one of them. They bring so much skill and experience to the job. When one pulls together a good crew, there is a sense of common purpose. We all feel a part of something larger than ourselves.

I am reminded of a moment when making *The Onion Field*. We were pushing hard to keep up with an almost impossible schedule. Time is a palpable presence, an invisible metronome that repeats "Don't fall behind" over and over. One day, I arrived at one of the courtrooms we were shooting in to find written in large letters on a white reflector board: "Shoot the film, not the schedule," a reminder from a crew member. It was their picture too!

Unlike most occupations, the work never repeats itself. The one abiding principle is that there is little room for error. You have to get it right the first time whether you're pulling focus or pushing a dolly.

Finally, the last day of the shoot arrived. We called wrap. It had been a marathon, and I returned to London exhausted. I booked into the Savoy for a few days' rest and slipped into the largest bathtub I had ever seen. I had to prop my foot against the faucet to keep from sliding under. The next morning, as I left my room, an old man in a wheelchair was coming down the long corridor. It was Charlie Chaplin. I surmise it was his wife, Oona, who was wheeling him. As they passed, I bowed to the legend.

Thirty days of film, hundreds of people involved, and now I was alone in a small suite of editing rooms with an editor and his assistant. I was fortunate in getting Tony Gibbs. He was not only a great editor, but he had edited *The Loneliness of the Long-Distance Runner*. I could only hope that some of it would rub off on our film.

When shooting wraps, the die is cast. Editing is when you find out if it works. If it holds together. Do all those reels, scene by scene, piece by piece, become a single entity? Hopefully, you end up with the movie you set out to make or even more.

The project had been a high-wire act from the very beginning. We were truly independent, but now we needed someone who believed in our film to distribute it. To get it out there so to speak.

Simply put, we needed a distributor to take a chance on an unknown director and a largely unknown cast.

And then we got our break. *The Ragman's Daughter* was chosen for the Venice Film Festival. It was a magical experience that began when we were put up at the Grand Hotel des Bains on the Lido. Luchino Visconti had shot *Death in Venice* (1971) at the hotel just a few years before, and the hotel was filled with the ghosts of that masterpiece. The dining room where Dirk Bogarde, who played the composer Gustav von Aschenbach, first sees the beautiful young boy Tadzio and becomes obsessed with him. The beach in front of the hotel where the composer dies, hair dye running down his face, Gustav Mahler's soaring score setting the tone. It was a surreal experience to be there with my first feature film, rubbing shoulders with ghosts.

I had met Silvana Mangano, who played Tadzio's mother, more than two decades earlier at Plucer's studio. Plucer was photographing her for *Vogue*, and I was starting my career as a photographer. She had a regal bearing, a far cry from the lusty young girl I had seen in *Bitter Rice* (1949) a few years earlier. I'd also met her husband, Dino de Laurentiis, who had produced two of my favorite films: *La Strada* (1954) and *Nights of Cabiria* (1957). Years later, our paths crossed again when he offered me a film to direct.

On the final night of the festival, we were anonymous in the crowd that filled the theater. The three of us—my producer Souter, my wife Susan, and I—were truly outsiders in this community of buyers, sellers, and filmmakers. They all seemed to know each other.

And then they announced that we had won the Donatello Award for Best First Feature. We were ecstatic. We finally felt like we belonged there.

Before the announcement

Donatello Award for Best First Feature

And After!

(Left to right) Souter Harris, Susan Becker, and Harold Becker

At the dinner that followed, swept away by the moment, I remember thinking, *What a great business this is*. Amazing how an award can produce temporary insanity.

We also got what we thought was a second bite of the apple when *Man Alive*, a BBC weekly show similar to *60 Minutes*, asked if they could cover us at Cannes, our next port of call. They explained that they were doing a show on the festival and wanted *The Ragman's Daughter*, an independent film, to be represented.

We were delighted. On our limited budget, any exposure was more than welcome.

As soon as we arrived in Cannes, we received a call from the producers of *Man Alive* asking Souter and me to join them on the Boulevard de la Croisette in front of the Carlton Cannes hotel.

Most of the heavyweights representing films at the festival were headquartered at the Carlton, a palatial five-star hotel well beyond our means. When we arrived, the *Man Alive* crew was waiting for us. They had set up two lounge chairs on the beach in front of the Carlton for our interview. They had framed the shot so that we appeared to be staying at the Carlton. We quickly realized that the whole thing had been planned that way, and we were just actors in a script they had written that had nothing to do with our reality.

It was only back in London, weeks later, when that episode of *Man Alive* aired that it all came into focus. Their "independent film" arrived by way of an attractive young woman who had bicycled all the way to Cannes from the airport, the "independent" 16mm film in her backpack. Talk about being "independent." There was no way to compete with that. The real star of the *Man Alive* episode was Sam Arkoff, a well-known American producer known for low-budget exploitation movies, who was a walking cliché of "the fat producer with a cigar." As he walked out of the airport surrounded by his entourage, his publicist's voice introduced him as "a gentleman in the true meaning of the word." The next cut was to Arkoff seated poolside at Hotel Du Cap selling a film about female cannibals.

The Ragman's Daughter opened in London in a single theater, which wasn't unusual for an independent release. The London reviews were good. There's always one you wish you would have been spared. I had been warned not to read reviews, but I couldn't help it. And, of course, you dwell on the negative ones. They seem to stick to you, at least for a while. It takes years to put it all in perspective, and by then it doesn't matter.

While in Cannes, I had met the film critic for *Women's Wear Daily*. She invited me to lunch, during which she explained to me how one became a newspaper film critic. It usually starts with a major in journalism, after which, if you're lucky enough to get a job, they start you on the local news, and if you don't get the names right, they put you on the entertainment page.

We had a modest opening. We were, after all, a small independent picture, and despite the award, we were swimming in a sea of big pictures starring big names and the advertising budgets to go with them.

***

With *The Ragman's Daughter*, I had a feature film to my credit, and now an agent, Roz Chatto, who also represented directors like Lindsey Anderson and Tony Richardson that I was proud to be on the card with. I was in good company.

All I could think of was my next film. I had read *After Leaving Mr. Mackenzie* by Jean Rhys, a haunting story of a woman adrift in Paris in the '30s, having left her lover, Mr. Mckenzie.

Rhys was living in the English countryside. She was still beautiful, an older version of Julia Martin, the novel's heroine. The book was clearly autobiographical, as were all of Jean Rhys's novels.

I thought of Julie Christie for the part—she was the embodiment of the character. I could see her walking the streets of Paris, or perhaps *haunting* the streets of Paris would be a better way of putting it.

Roz Chatto sent the screenplay to Julie, who was living in Los Angeles at the time. I later learned from David Naylor, a friend who was involved with her at the time, that she had been interested and had even gone out of her way to see *The Ragman's Daughter*, but simply didn't want to leave LA.

I offered the part of Mr. Mckenzie to Alan Bates. It was a small but pivotal role that he would have been perfect for, but he turned it down. Miriam Brickman, who was helping me with the casting, explained the obvious: "Actors count their lines."

I was able to interest Susannah York, whose starring roles in *Tom Jones* (1963) and *They Shoot Horses, Don't They?* (1969) had made her an international star. But it was to no avail. I was facing the hard reality of the marketplace. Yes, I had made a film that had won an award and received some good notices, but it didn't make money. That was the gold standard.

I had a script based on the work of a highly-praised author and the interest of a movie star, but it simply wasn't commercial. It was a dark story, a story of loneliness and despair. Yes, it was haunting and poetic—that's what had drawn me to it—but even on the small budget we would make it on, studios simply didn't see the return.

Another factor that was clouding the horizon was the '60s, which were filled with promise, were over. England was tipping into a recession. In the wake of the darker times, the tightening up, American filmmakers were pulling up their stakes as well. What had been a vibrant American global presence in cinema had pretty much decamped. Even though I wasn't part of that American presence, I felt the whiplash as well.

I returned to New York. A welcome back dinner at the Ninth Street Steakhouse, an old hangout, with a group of friends talking about films. In retrospect, what made the dinner memorable was the presence of a young producer, Jerry Bruckheimer, who I had done some commercials with. Jerry was something of a wunderkind, still in his twenties producing commercials at BBDO for major advertisers. He announced that he was departing for the promised land—he was going to Hollywood to produce *The Culpepper Cattle Co.* (1972) for Dick Richards. He was on his way.

The Ragman's Daughter had a cursory release in the States, despite my efforts to give it a theatrical presence. I remember a call from Penelope Gilliatt, a writer and one of the film critics for *The New Yorker*, asking me to send her the script, as she was going to be reviewing my film. I thought this was unusual, but I was so happy to be getting reviewed, I dutifully showed up at her doorstep to deliver the script. The door half opened, a hand reached out and took the script, and the door closed. That was it. Well, I guess it beat her having to go to the Festival Cinema on Fifty-Seventh Street where the picture was playing just a few blocks away. I don't remember her review, if there ever was one. I regretted having acceded to her request; after all, she was supposed to be reviewing a film, not a screenplay, but it was a sign of my desperation at the time.

Now that we were in the '70s, the pendulum had swung back. Young American filmmakers were being heard from. Francis Ford Coppola's masterpiece *The Godfather* came out in 1972. Billy Friedkin burst onto the scene with a one-two punch with *The French Connection* (1971) and *The Exorcist* (1973). Of course, American films had always been a benchmark, but the '50s and '60s had seen a breathtaking post-war renaissance in European cinema. The '70s brought a new spirit in American filmmaking. Maybe the European Renaissance had inspired it. Small independent films were beginning to make their presence felt.

The Panic in Needle Park (1971) with Al Pacino, who had made an indelible impression on me when I saw him on the stage in *The Indian Wants the Bronx* in 1967, gave me some hope. The film was directed by Jerry Schatzberg, who had also been a still photographer in New York and a contemporary of mine. The cinematographer,

Adam Holender, was a close friend. It was made on a small budget but filled with talent; it was the kind of independent film I aspired to create.

And then a serendipitous event occurred. Once again, the unexpected changed everything. I had been spending more of my time on the West Coast. This was where the film business was. This was the marketplace. I was meeting new people and reconnecting with some I knew from New York. I screened *Ragman* for them. A few of them saw its merits, but none of them could place it in the context of the world I was trying to enter.

Then one day, I ran into Ronda Gomez. She was an agent at Adams, Ray & Rosenberg, a boutique agency. She was also the girlfriend of a good friend and filmmaker from New York, Howard Zieff. Howard had had a great career as a still photographer and had moved into commercials, much as I had. Now he was in Hollywood making feature films. His first, *Slither* (1973), had sent him on his way.

Knowing I didn't have an agent here, Ronda suggested I let her represent me. Getting an agent out here seemed alien to me. I was still thinking of making films outside the studio system. But finally, I took her up on her offer and, within three months, I had a call from Lee Rosenberg, the head of Rhonda's agency. Lee had introduced Joseph Wambaugh to my work, and Joe was interested in meeting to talk about me directing *The Onion Field*.

CHAPTER 12
THE ONION FIELD (1979)

The Onion Field is Joseph Wambaugh's nonfiction account of the kidnapping of two plainclothes LAPD officers during a traffic stop and the subsequent murder of one of the officers. It was a great work of nonfiction, and Joe was already a legend in Hollywood. A best-selling author and ex-cop, Joe's books *The New Centurions*, *The Blue Knight*, and *The Choirboys* had been made into successful films and a TV series.

How did I measure up? What in my work or background attracted Joe to think that I was capable of bringing his book to the screen? I had read the book, and it only raised my doubts about whether I was up to the task. God knows nothing in my background had prepared me for it. Yes, I had made a gritty film about a young working-class kid that didn't pull its punches, but it was a far cry from the unremitting darkness of *The Onion Field*. In fact, I had called Lee Rosenberg to cancel the meeting, only to be met by his fateful words: "Do you have anything better to do?"

Lee arranged for me to meet Joe at a roadhouse called Tail o' the Cock, which was halfway between my hotel in Beverly Hills and Joe's home in San Marino. It was mid-afternoon, and we had the cavernous place to ourselves, except for the occasional couple hidden away in one of the booths.

Joe and his wife, Dee, were already there when I arrived. First impressions are often lasting ones, and the one I had of Joe, straight as an arrow, has stayed with me. His first words to me were, "If I was born to do one thing in my life, it was to write *The Onion Field*." Indeed, he had written a masterpiece, and it was those words that made me want to be a part of it, to bring his vision to the screen. Whatever my doubts, I was swept up by his passion.

And so we began. He had written the script and would be the sole writer. He would be at my side, and he said to me at the outset, "I would no more think of telling you how to direct than I would think of you telling me how to write." I've never struck a better bargain. He prophetically continued, "You may not have all the money you need, but you will have more creative freedom than you will ever have again in this town."

Joe's first draft came in at close to two hundred pages. We knew we had our work cut out for us, but we finally trimmed it down to a manageable hundred and twenty-something pages. I knew that if we ever got the money to make the film it would be on a very tight budget. Joe was determined to make it independent of the studios because he wanted us to have complete control. It was a dark story, a tragic one. There was never a thought of compromising to make it more commercial. We knew it would be a hard film to watch. We couldn't think about that. The book was our bible, and staying true to it was our mantra. It was the driving force that gave this dark tale its power. As Joe said to me at the outset, "The most important five words in this script are 'this is a true story.'"

A film that had traveled the road we were taking was *In Cold Blood*, Richard Brooks's brilliant docudrama, based on Truman Capote's classic work of nonfiction. Its bleak, unerring look into the heart of darkness was an inspiration to me.

As to the independent financing, it started with the half-a-million-dollar settlement that Columbia Pictures paid Joe for breaking a contract they had made with him when he sold them the rights to *The Choir Boys*. Joe wrote the script, and Columbia agreed to the proviso that they couldn't change a word in the script without his consent.

Robert Aldrich, the director, had the script rewritten without consulting Joe. In fact, when meeting with the group of young actors in the film at the start of production, Aldrich swore them all to secrecy. I am confounded to this day that he thought he could compel over twenty actors to keep a secret. I've always been of the opinion that if two people share a secret, that's one too many. In any case, the half-million settlement was a start.

Dee raised the rest of the two million dollars, which was the minimum we thought we needed, from private investors. She had never done fundraising like that before, yet she pulled off a miracle.

Joe called in a favor from a major line producer, asking him to create a budget for the film. The line producer came by to pick up the script, then before leaving, he turned and said, "By the way, how much money do you have?" We told him we had two million dollars, and he replied, "Then I'll give you a two-million-dollar budget."

The budget called for a forty-day shoot. Twenty days and twenty nights. It was going to be a marathon. There was no coming up for air, our schedule often calling for shooting two scenes a day, sometimes in different locations. And so we got to work.

In discussing the credits, Joe suggested I take the producer credit on top of director. I pointed out that the producer credit was his; after all, he had not only written the book and the screenplay, he had raised the money as well. But Joe only wanted the writing credit.

That's how Walter Coblenz entered the picture. He was an experienced producer with a background as a line producer and seemed to be just what we needed. As soon as he was on board, he started giving us orders. That's not what we had in mind. We sorted it out—or at least we thought we had, but more on that later.

My biggest challenge was the casting. Needless to say, after the script, casting is everything. The alpha and omega. It's where films go to die when they don't get it right. When you get it right, you can't imagine it being otherwise.

Lynn Stalmaster, arguably one of the most prominent casting directors in Hollywood, agreed to cast our film. After having Miriam Brickman cast my first feature, I felt my luck was holding. However, after a few initial meetings with Lynn, I realized he had a lot on his plate, and the real day-to-day work was being done by two of his assistants, Toni Howard and Nancy Klopper. *The Onion Field* was the first of many films Nancy and I worked on together.

In casting the leading role, we had one major asset: We didn't need stars to secure financing. Our only criteria was: "Are they right for the part?"

Coblenz had rented us a space in the old Technicolor building in Hollywood. While showing us the space, he made it clear that he was going to occupy the large corner office, leaving the smaller offices for Joe and myself. It didn't endear me to him when I insisted on taking the larger space. It wasn't ego; it was the only room large enough for us to tape auditions.

There were four people on that fatal ride to the onion field. The two cops, one of whom would not return, and the killers. Gregory Powell, the criminal who pulled the trigger, was the driving force in our narrative. I needed an actor who could step into Powell's shoes, who could become him. When James "Jimmy" Woods auditioned for the part, the first thing he told me was that he was wrong for the role. He stated that he didn't look anything like Powell, who was living in a cell in San Quentin, just a few hundred miles away.

Jimmy was brilliant. He knew what we were thinking. He was right when he said he didn't look anything like Powell, who was blonde and had icy blue eyes that could put a chill through you. Jimmy had dark brown hair and brown eyes. He anticipated my concern as he pointed out the obvious to me. It was a brilliant ploy, and it reminded me to look past his looks to his obvious talent.

That same day, another very talented actor auditioned, and like Powell, he had blonde hair and icy blue eyes. He stepped right into Powell's shoes. When he left the audition, Joe came running in. He had seen the actor as he was leaving and excitedly told me he had just seen Gregory Powell. I agreed, but told him that I had seen another actor that I thought was even better, though he didn't look the part.

I knew that the only way to convince Joe—and maybe myself—was to do a screen test. The rest is history. James Woods was Gregory Powell to the core. He was the driving force of our film.

An indelible lesson: Go with the talent, and the rest will follow.

Almost all of the film was shot on location, much of it on the actual locations where it had taken place. As though haunted by its past, the streets had hardly changed since that fatal night.

At the intersection of Gower Street and Carlos Avenue in Hollywood, Ian Campbell and Karl Hettinger, two plainclothes officers on patrol, pull over a car driven by Powell with his accomplice Jimmy Lee Smith in the shotgun seat. In a tragic turn of events, Powell gets the draw on Campbell, and the criminals force the cops into the car, beginning the ride to the onion field. We filmed on the freeway that the actual journey took place on.

When we got to the onion field, the tension was palpable. I can still feel the cold chill that went through me in the middle of that field. The stillness, the smell of onions, the foreboding darkness that enveloped us. It was as though we were reliving that terrible moment again.

When James Woods stepped out of the car and "shot" Ted Danson (playing Campbell) in the face point blank, Woods's partner, Franklyn Seales (playing Smith), started screaming. That's how real it felt to him—how real it felt to all of us. His screaming was unscripted. It's there on the soundtrack forever. It brought it to life for all of us, the cast and the crew. Talk about being in the moment. That's what it felt like. It still does.

We didn't make *The Onion Field*, we lived it.

Out of respect for my principal actors, I had private screenings for each of them when the film was finished. This was Ted Danson's first film, and when he saw the closeup of himself being shot in the face, it was too much for him. He jumped up and ran out of the theater. It was a couple of years before he could bring himself to see the entire film.

Another of my leads making his debut was Franklyn Seales. He brought such pathos to his role as a born loser manipulated and controlled by a raging psychopath, especially with his final epitaph: "I was born for a prison yard."

And then there was John Savage, who was already an established presence with major roles in *The Deer Hunter* (1978) and *Hair* (1979). He played Hettinger, the lone officer to survive that tragic night, only to suffer the guilt of a survivor. As Joe Wambaugh put it, "What happened in the Onion Field is true, but the real crime is what happened after."

Back to our "producer" Walter Coblenz. About two weeks into the shoot, he called Joe and me into an urgent meeting. The film editor and the production designer, Brian Eatwell, were also present. I had known Brian since my days in London and considered him a friend. It was unusual to be meeting after a long day on location.

Walter got right to the point. Looking straight at me, he said "I think you should be replaced immediately. The film you're shooting can never be cut together."

According to him, I was not shooting enough coverage. Brian and the editor agreed. In fact, Walter informed Joe that he had a replacement ready to step in.

I sat there in shocked silence. There I was surrounded by the "pros." It is true that I was not shooting the scenes in a conventional manner—establishing shot, medium shot, etc. There's no way I could shoot two or more scenes a day using this method. Nor did this way of working interest me. My God, by the time you got to the close ups, it would have lost all spontaneity, all of the feeling of the reality I was striving for. I came up with the idea of shooting a moving master. I started with an establishing shot and moved into the close-up in one take. That way, with perhaps one reverse, I had the scene covered. There was no point in trying to explain this to

Joe. This was not his area of expertise, and we were surrounded by "experts."

I'll never forget that night, going home numb. I was still in shock when the phone rang. It was Joe apologizing for not speaking up sooner. He had never for a moment doubted me. Relief flooded through me. I'll never be able to repay Joe for that call. In a strange way, that vote of confidence filled me with an even stronger sense of purpose.

We had a young crew, many of whom had cut their teeth on commercials as I had. But what they lacked in experience, they more than made up for in their commitment. They felt, as did everyone on that set, that they were part of something special.

That message to me in the courthouse, "Shoot the film, not the schedule," summed it up.

We lacked the money for the cranes and the Wendy lights to illuminate our onion field. Tim Evans, our gaffer, ingeniously lit the field by laying headlights along the rows of onions. We made do with what we had, and in retrospect, it only added to the dark drama we were filming.

As I mentioned, our schedule called for twenty days and twenty nights. The nights were the hard part. They would begin at about six p.m. when we still had some light, and we would try to have as much of the night work done before we broke for dinner at midnight. The few hours after that were tough going. The actual onion fields were in Bakersfield, which was hours away. We made do with the fields in Valencia, only an hour away. We were surrounded by acres of onions fields that didn't know the difference.

While we were not allowed to shoot at San Quentin, where Powell and Smith were incarcerated, I visited the prison with my cinematographer and production designer. Since San Quentin was off limits, we recreated a facsimile of the areas we needed at a local prison that was no longer in use.

Our trip to San Quentin was an unforgettable experience, which began in the reception area. We were required to sign a waiver that made clear that if we were held hostage, the authorities would not negotiate for our release. Though I can understand the reason for it—they didn't want visitors to become bait—it still put a chill through me. Though it did help me to create the prison scene when the condemned walked through the general population and the guard repeats "Dead man walking" over and over, as well as the harrowing scenes on death row.

After twenty days and twenty nights, we had a film but no distributor. After seeing the first rough cut, Joe was so full of enthusiasm for the film that, without my knowing it, he had arranged a screening for the four major studios. We hadn't even put in the sound effects. Watching a car speed around a corner without the sound of screeching tires made it look as though it was going twenty miles an hour instead of sixty. Nonetheless, the film worked. Those were the key words. I remember Walter Coblenz, walking out of the screening room dumbfounded, saying, "It works." He was proud to present it at his alma mater, the University of Texas.

Within a week of showing the picture to the studios, we had been turned down by all of them. Yes, many of them called to praise the film, but none of them thought it was worth gambling on. It's a lot safer to say no. It's risk free. Sherry Lansing, then an assistant to Daniel Melnick, who was the head of Columbia Pictures at the time, expressed her enthusiasm for the film. Later, she told me that she had been admonished by Melnick. He didn't want to raise our hopes that they would release our film. We did get a small distributor, Embassy, who agreed to a limited release. They put up a minuscule budget of one million dollars for prints and advertisement. It amounted to an eighth-of-a-page ad in the Friday edition of *The New York Times*. Hardly noticeable in a newspaper that was filled with full-page ads for films opening that weekend.

We opened at the Murray Hill, one of the indie cinemas in New York. I had been told that it was usual for the director to drop by on opening night. When I got to the theater, I was stunned to see a long line waiting to buy tickets. It was so far beyond our expectations.

Unbeknownst to me, Joe had written a screenplay for another one of his books, *The Black Marble*, a black comedy that he asked me to direct. He assured me that we were going to make back the money we were about to lose on *The Onion Field*.

Fortunately, it didn't work out that way. *The Onion Field* was a hit. A small hit, but a hit nonetheless. It made back many times its cost, but most importantly, it changed my life.

CHAPTER 13
THE BLACK MARBLE (1980)

The Black Marble is a romantic comedy that only Joe Wambaugh could have written. It is funny, painful, and romantic—often at the same time. It centers on a mismatched couple of detectives, played by Paula Prentiss and Robert Foxworth, tracking down a hapless dognapper, played by the uniquely talented Harry Dean Stanton, who was always a memorable presence in whatever he did.

I couldn't believe my luck in getting Owen Roizman, a great cinematographer with credits like *The French Connection* (1971), *The Exorcist* (1973), and other major films under his belt, to film *The Black Marble*. In the opening scene, which we shot in a Greek Orthodox Church in El Segundo, Owen's lighting made a church the size of a matchbox look like a cathedral. I had chosen the church because it had a magnificent altar lit by dozens of candles that reflected the jeweled robes of the priests. Owen's lighting made it appear as though the entire church was lit by candles.

Each film opens new vistas. In *The Black Marble*, it was dog shows—a world unto itself. The dog owners, the dog groomers, the rituals of the dogs on display vying for the gold. We created our own dog show. Up went the tents, the arena with its grandstand filled with contestants and their dogs, and at the center of it all, our dognapper, Harry Dean Stanton. Desperation oozed out of him as he carried out his wild scheme.

The Black Marble is filled with black humor, with Barbara Babcock in a jewel of a performance playing the desperate owner of a kidnapped schnauzer. I even brought in James Woods for a cameo playing a roaming fiddler providing romantic background music for a scene between our two stars.

While "clothes make the man" might be overstating it, in the hands of my brilliant costume designer, Susan Becker, clothes *did* make the man. Stanton's wardrobe went a long way in establishing "Philo, the Terrier King." From the skintight tie-dye shirts open to his navel, to his white belt with loafers to match, it brilliantly spelled out the character of the Terrier King before a word was spoken.

Susan and Harold Becker

Despite a wonderful cast and good reviews, *The Black Marble* was out of theaters within a couple of weeks. I remembered a film critic for *The Philadelphia Inquirer* who interviewed me while I was shooting my next project, *Taps*, outside of Philadelphia. He took me to task for the short run, as though I had any control over it. He was a fan of *The Black Marble* and had arranged a double-page spread in *The Inquirer* when it opened in Philly. Unfortunately, the film was gone by the time they published it. As the saying goes, "black comedies open on Friday and close on Sunday." The exception, of course, was for films blessed with "star power." We had terrific actors in Robert Foxworth, Paula Prentiss, and Harry Dean

Stanton—as good as I could have wished for. But what we didn't have was Cary Grant and Katharine Hepburn, movie stars who could turn a screwball comedy like *Bringing Up Baby* (1938), which featured a pet leopard, into a classic hit of its genre.

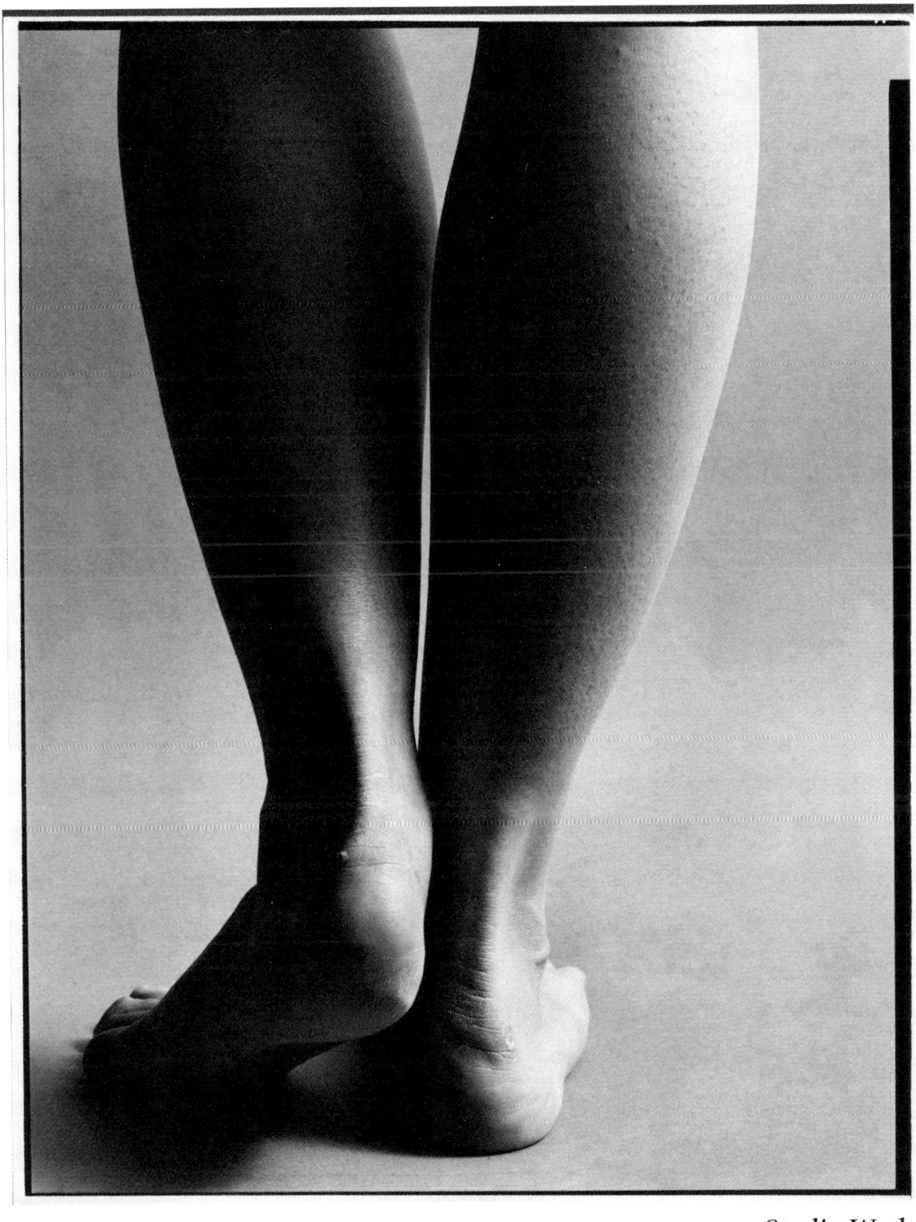

Studio Work

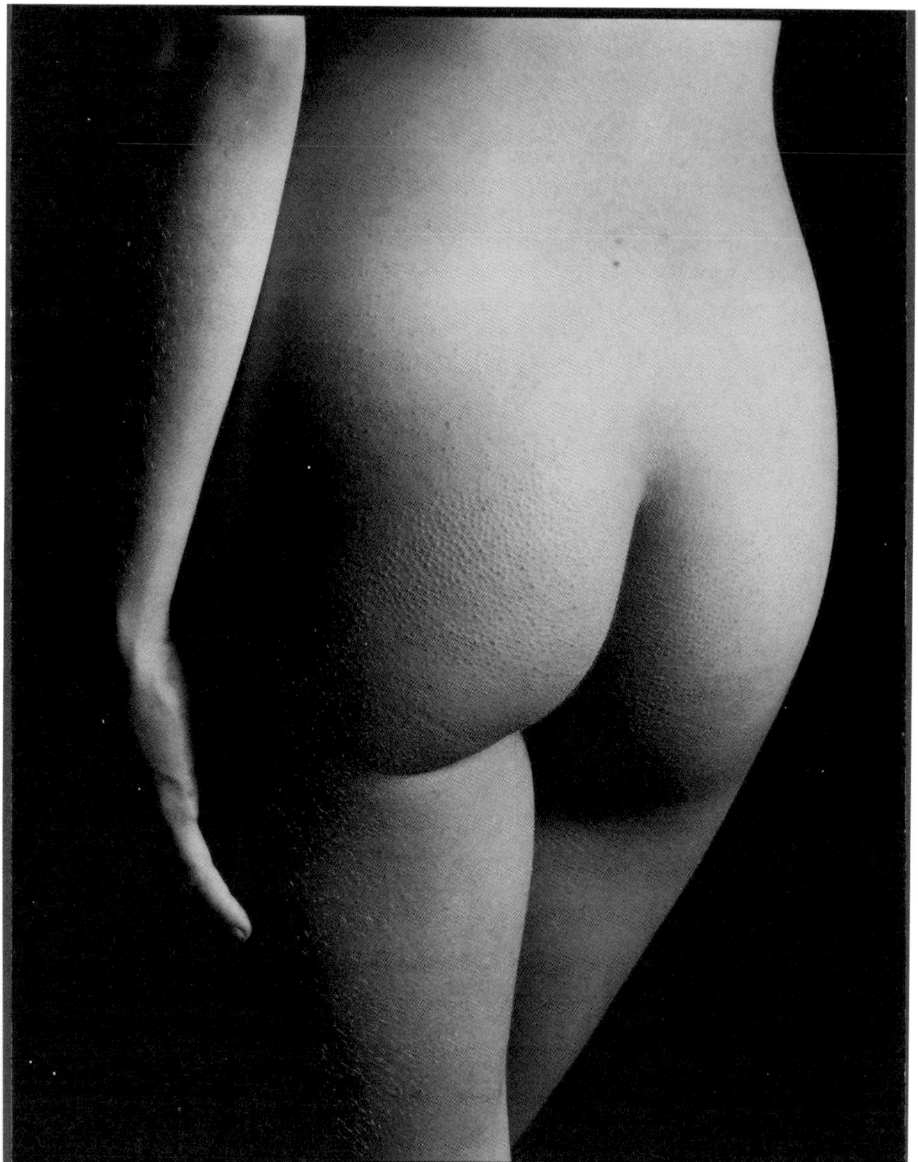

Greece

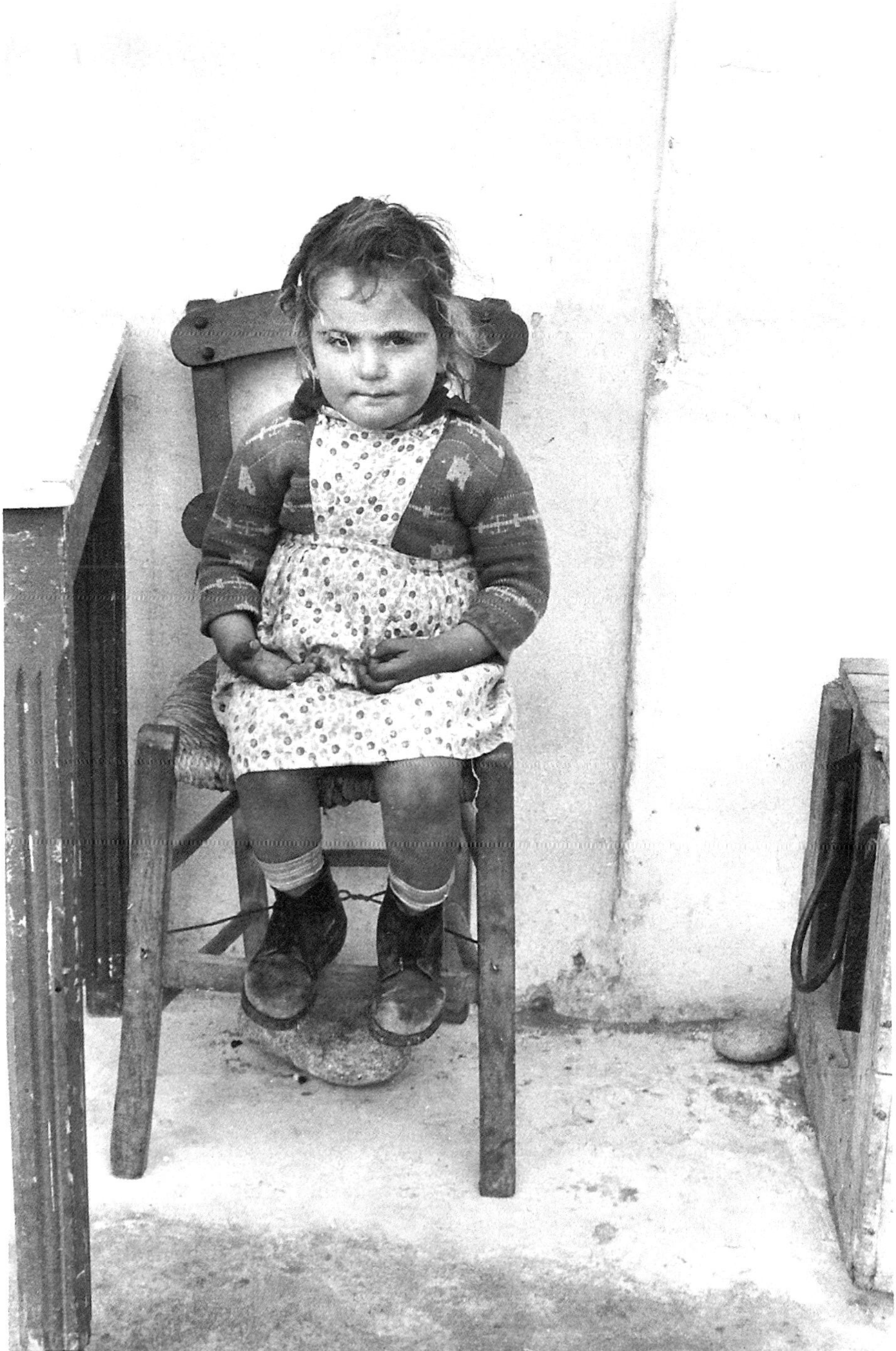

Italy

USA

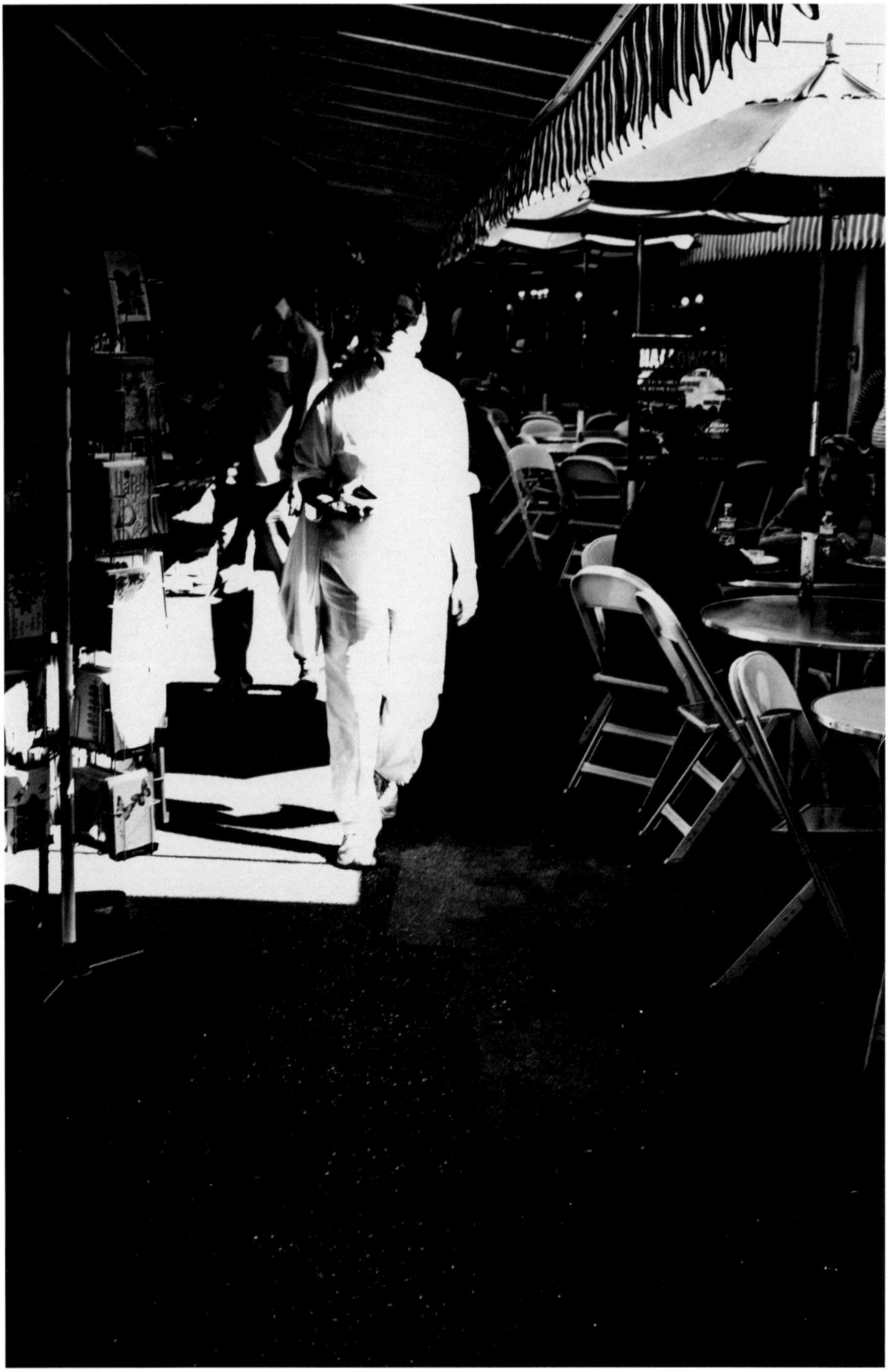

Farmers Market
Poultry
TEA
SHORT

4A

CHAPTER 14
TAPS
(1981)

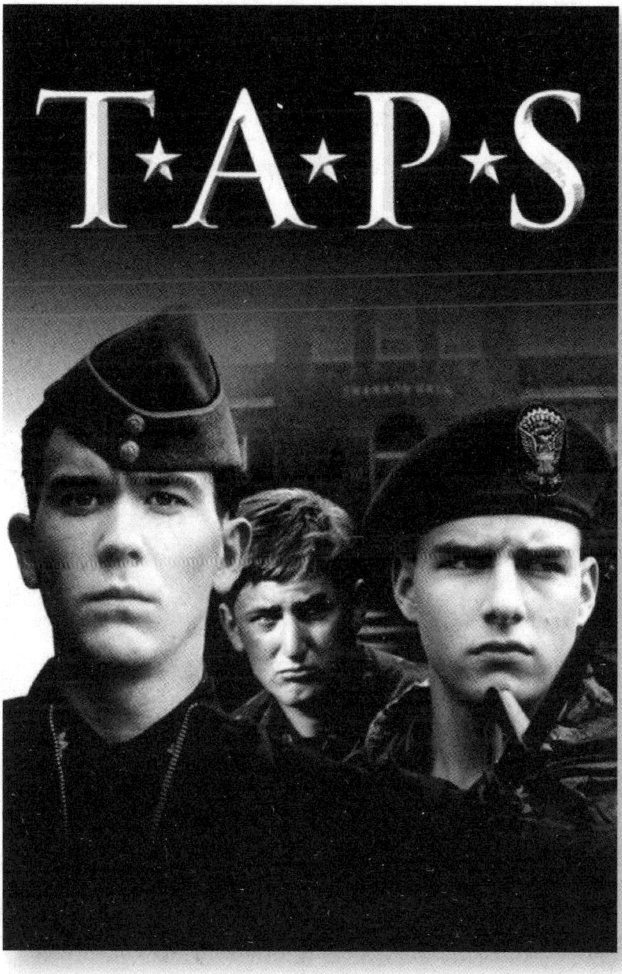

My first studio picture was *Taps*. Stanley Jaffe, a major producer, offered me the picture after seeing *The Onion Field*.

I was in Stanley's office when he called Frank Price, the head of Columbia Pictures, where *Taps* was going to be made, with the news that he had chosen me to direct. Obviously, Frank Price must have asked him who the hell was Harold Becker. Stanley told him I had directed *The Onion Field*. The rest is surmised—I only heard one side of the conversation. Price must have asked Stanley to send him the film so he could judge for himself. Stanley hung up on him, and the next thing I knew, he had moved the picture to Fox. That was Stanley in a nutshell and the beginning of a great relationship.

Stanley was passionate and combustible, but it was always about the picture. Unlike *The Onion Field*, *Taps* was a work of fiction. We couldn't have the all-important words "This is a true story" above the title. We had to make it *feel* like a true story.

The story of teenage cadets taking over a military academy and defying the troops sent in to quell the armed rebellion strains credibility. It was our job to make it believable, starting with the script. We tried to anchor it in reality from the retired half-mad general, who ran the academy as if he was still in the military and that was his command, to his young acolytes, the cadets who he filled with an untethered romantic idealism.

I brought in Darryl Ponicsan to write the screenplay. His credits included *Cinderella Liberty* (1973) and *The Last Detail* (1973), both based on novels he had written. *Taps* was based on the novel *Father Sky* by Devery Freeman. Darryl took it from there.

We set the film at the Valley Forge Military Academy and used their cadets as extras. I asked for six weeks of rehearsal so I could meld my cast—many of whom, including two of my principals, had never been in front of a camera before—seamlessly into the cadet corps of the real academy. It gave further credence to our film.

I referred to our rehearsals as an officer training program. Even when my actors were on the parade grounds marching in tight formation, they were indistinguishable from the real cadets.

As usual, casting was critical. Our drama centered around the impressionable young cadets who led the corps and General Harlan Bache, the general who headed the academy, played by George C. Scott. Casting George as the head of the academy was pivotal. His iconic portrayal of General George S. Patton in *Patton* (1970) made our story even more credible. He was the linchpin that made it all work. Casting Timothy "Tim" Hutton as Cadet Major Brian Moreland had been relatively simple since I had been privileged to see scenes from his upcoming film, *Ordinary People* (1980). I knew I had one my leads.

Shirley Rich, my casting director, was well-steeped in the New York theater scene. Most of her work had been for the stage. She recommended I see *Heartland*, an off-Broadway play. The lead was a young actor named Sean Penn. Again, I felt that I had struck gold. When he came in for the audition, Stanley was in the room with me. Without much ado, Sean upended the audition by doing a magic trick. We didn't bother asking him to read. He was magic.

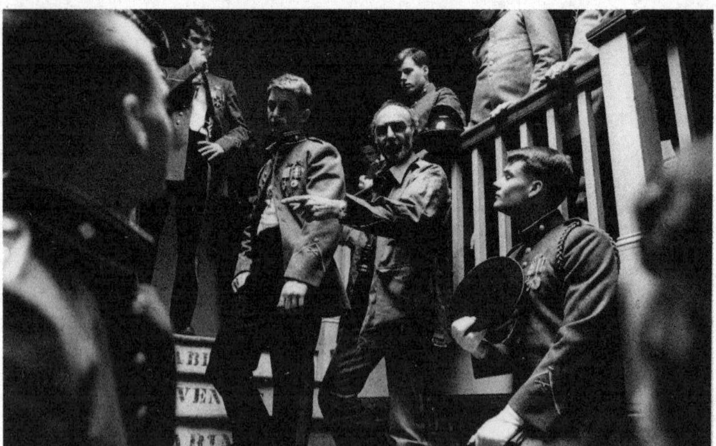

Finding my third lead proved more difficult. I had initially cast a talented young actor from Nashville, but during the rehearsal weeks, we discovered that he didn't measure up. The part called for what the General would have referred to as having "fire in the belly," which he would claim is what it took to command. The young actor, though talented, didn't have that. After weeks of rehearsal, I knew I had to replace him.

While casting my principals, I'd also cast a group of extras—foreground players, you might call them—that I could throw a line to here or there. I noticed one of them who really stood out. He had an intensity and a charisma, and he seemed perfect for the part. I remember the impression he made on me, seeing him on the parade ground. He was literally leading the corps. Here was a kid who could walk through walls. His name was Tom Cruise.

I called Tom into my office and explained the situation. I was replacing one of my leads. Unfortunately, he was wrong for the part, and so I offered the role to Tom. Without skipping a beat, he turned it down. Here was the opportunity of a lifetime—to go from being an extra to a lead. But for Tom, the overriding issue was that he didn't want to take a role away from somebody else, someone who had become a friend. I remember thinking that I wouldn't experience this again. I explained that I would find another part for the other actor, and if Tom wasn't going to take the part, I would be taking the next train back to New York to recast it. It was only then that he relented.

The idea of the National Guard firing on teenage cadets seemed so preposterous that it undermined the believability of our story, so I sought to support it with some precedent. I immediately thought about an incident at Kent State University On May 4, 1970, the National Guard had fired on unarmed students, killing four of them.

We wove that into our script. For me, it was a critical reference. Unfortunately, we knew that the National Guard, which was supplying us with tanks and other armaments for our climactic last scene, would not be pleased with that reference, so we omitted it from the script we sent them to review. Stanley entrusted one of the associate producers to make sure the "right" script was sent to the Guard. We even went so far as putting a different-colored cover on the script we wanted sent to the Guard.

I'll never forget the look on Stanley's face when he broke the news to me. The Guard had been sent the wrong script, the one we didn't want them to see. Without the Guard's support, we ended up renting the equipment we needed. The line about Kent State was worth it.

Having George Scott as the half-mad general who heads the academy and fills the young cadets with dreams of martial glory was the key to it all. He had the weight and the charisma to pull it off. My young cast were in his thrall.

What really endeared me to George, besides his obvious talent, was his relationship with his young cadets, Tim, Sean, and Tom. Despite his accomplishments, there was no conceit; he treated his young charges as equals, as fellow actors. I would often see him on the set playing chess with my young actors while waiting to go on.

Exercising some control over ten or twenty young people in their late teens or early twenties, many of whom had never been on their own before, was no easy task.

There was the three a.m. call when one of my cadets had "reordered" the lobby of the hotel he was staying in after being rejected by a young receptionist. Fortunately for me, it fell on the shoulders of my producer to restore order when the early-morning calls came in from the hotel or the police about egregious behavior on the part of one or more of our cadets. Stanley handled it. It would have been a twenty-four-hour day without that.

It was a long shoot, made even longer by a Screen Actors Guild (SAG) strike that delayed the start of principle photography for a couple of months, so we were still shooting when that year's Academy Award nominations were announced. Tim Hutton was nominated for his role in *Ordinary People*. We adjusted our schedule so he could attend the ceremony, where he won for Best Supporting Actor. He was the youngest recipient for that award in the history of the Academy.

We were overjoyed, but I remember George expressing some reservations. Not about Tim deserving the award, but more his concern with the weight of the award on such a young actor. George's aversion to awards was well-known. He felt that the whole process was little more than a meat market. He never even showed up to accept a well-deserved Oscar for his performance in *Patton*. Awards can be a burden as well as a blessing.

Not long after Tim returned, we received a call from his agent requesting that Tim be given his own trailer as befit his new status. We had deliberately created a level playing field for our actors, from their accommodations to their treatment on set. It was all part of creating a parallel world to the real campus we were shooting on.

We had to accommodate the demand, but it did isolate Tim from the others. I would often see Tim sitting alone in his trailer signing headshots. He had gone to the awards a cadet and returned a celebrity. Fortunately, it was late in the shoot and there was already a sense of camaraderie, a sense of being a part of something, a sense of mission, that had my cadets marching in step before the final credits rolled.

You don't make a film of this scope without a lot of support. Owen Roizman, my cinematographer, was a steady hand at the wheel. This was our second film together, and he brought a terrific crew with him, a group of craftsmen, grips, gaffers, and more. One can't underestimate what a group like this brings to a production. They were pros. I can't think of higher praise.

Taps (1981)

I'm thinking of the day we were set to shoot the climactic last scene: Sean Penn carrying Tim Hutton in his arms, exiting the battle-scarred barracks. I had planned it as a helicopter shot that would start on Sean carrying Tim's body through the doorway into the street, and as they moved towards the camera that we had mounted on a helicopter, the helicopter would slowly rise and carry us into a wide shot that encompassed the scene of the battle as Sean moved away from us. It was the final shot of the film. Owen and I had rehearsed the camera moves many times and waited for the sun to set. I wanted the ending shot playing against the setting sun.

When the time arrived, we were prepared. The helicopter blades were spinning, ready to take us up as Sean approached, carrying a mortally wounded Tim. Then the unexpected occurred: The powerful wind generated from the helicopter blades blew Sean back into the doorway as though he was headed into a windstorm.

Sadly, we had to abandon the helicopter, but here is where Owen and a great crew come in. We realized we had to do it as a crane shot, and we had to do it fast. The sun was setting. Within minutes, Owen's crew had the crane in place, and we were able to get our shot.

One can't underestimate the importance of the support from a great cinematographer. From the lighting to the framing, Owen and I were in sync. Yes, I was a very experienced photographer myself, but it was more than that. It was how we collaborated to organize the day's work, the rhythm we established. Owen brought years of experience from working on major productions.

The day started with rehearsals, the blocking, the stand-ins, so Owen could do his work while the cast went to costume and make-up. It flowed smoothly. Each person knew their job and how to fit in so that when I called action, everything fell into place.

Taps was a large canvas, larger than any I had worked on. Owen's steady hand was crucial to its success.

As I write this, I have just learned of Owen's passing. We did three films together—*The Black Marble*, *Taps*, and *Vision Quest*. His presence, his talent, and his friendship blessed all of them.

Working with talented people is one of the joys of filmmaking. Their mastery raises everybody's game. There are no politics, no distractions—it's all about the work. You spark off of each other.

When an editor puts two pieces of film together in a way you hadn't anticipated, you're reminded how fortunate you are to be working with others who are so good at their job.

There's a scene in *City Hall* where, again working with a great editor Bob Jones, we had a wide shot of a train speeding across the horizon. It just lay there inert until Bob cut to a close up of the same train. A simple cut and the scene came to life.

And who better than Maurice Jarre to score the film. Maurice, who had scored many of David Lean's films, was a brilliant composer and was particularly adept in creating scores that had a martial air, such as his scores for *Lawrence of Arabia* (1962) and *The Bridge on the River Kwai* (1957). Again, I was walking in the footsteps of masters.

Jarre's score was everything I could have hoped for—except for one cue. An important one. In the confrontation between the cadets and the national guard, the tension builds to a terrible moment when a cadet is shot. We needed to score the scene so that it would build to that moment. It's the kind of tension music we've heard a million times over in films. Unfortunately, it wasn't in our score, and Maurice was in Europe.

Stanley called in a favor. John Williams—yes, the great John Williams—at that moment, was at a recording studio and graciously agreed to help us out. He told Stanley he would record a cue for us at the end of his recording session.

Stanley and I were in the recording studio waiting for John to finish. He had tacked on extra time to record the cue he had written for us. We waited with bated breath as he began. It was a great cue. Unfortunately, we felt we had heard it before. It was remarkably similar to the famous cue John had written for *Jaws*. We looked at each other. Finally, Stanley said, "I think you better go up there and talk to John." I was wishing Stanley would, but it was my call. I had to go out there and face John Williams, who I hardly knew. After a long, uncomfortable moment while he waited for my reaction, I finally got it out. Like the pro he was, he amended the cue.

Taps, which was made on a modest budget for a film of its size and scope, did well at the box office. It was particularly successful with teenagers who could readily identify with their counterparts on the screen. They cheered for the cadets' rebellion and, for a couple of hours, they were a part of it. Even today, many of those teenagers, now in their forties and fifties, seek me out to share their memories of seeing *Taps*.

Taps was my real entry to Hollywood. Though I had already made three feature films, they had all been done independently, outside the studio system. *Taps* checked all the boxes. It had a major producer, it had a bona fide studio, it came in on budget, and it made money. It also introduced two young actors who went on to major careers.

The Onion Field had caught Hollywood's attention, but it was an outlier—an unremittingly dark view of the human condition best left to independent filmmakers.

Thanks *to Taps*, a new world opened to me. I was invited in. Warner Bros. gave me a studio deal and offices. It became my new home.

CHAPTER 15
VISION QUEST (1985)

Warner Bros. sent me a novel by Terry Davis that was ostensibly about a high school wrestler named Louden Swain, but it was so much more. It was a spiritual journey, hence the title *Vision Quest*, as well as a coming of age story. I brought in Darryl Ponicsan, who had done *Taps* with me, to write the screenplay.

The producers on the project, Peter Guber and Jon Peters, had a major production deal at Warners. Unlike Stanley Jaffe, who did one picture at a time, they had many projects in the works. They were literally a studio within the studio. This had its advantages, specifically that I had more freedom. The downside was that I didn't have the hands-on support that Stanley provided. I did develop a close relationship with Jon Peters, but he was a horse of a different color.

Jon was a larger-than-life character, rough around the edges but charismatic. He had a great rags-to-riches story, and he loved telling it. He came from a family of hairdressers, and he started off dyeing showgirls' "muffs" to match their hair color while he was still a teenager. He was soon the hairdresser to Hollywood stars. Barbra Streisand was his entrée to the film world. Where but in Hollywood does a muff dyer end up as a major producer?

By the time we met, he and Guber had a string of hits and misses. They weren't that involved on the creative side, which suited me fine. We were going to be shooting in Spokane, Washington, and I knew Jon wouldn't be spending much time there.

Their background was very helpful on the music side. They had originally been partners in PolyGram Records and knew their way around that world. One of the key scenes in *Vision Quest* took place at a roadhouse. It's a backdrop for a romantic moment in the film, and we needed a singer for the scene.

I was looking for a local girl because I certainly didn't want to bring in a ringer. I felt it would undermine the believability of the story. To me, the singer was part of the background to the scene. Jon urged me to consider a young singer from New York who was already getting attention—Madonna. I had seen her in a small club in New York. She was the real thing. Still relatively unknown at the time, she fit right in.

She performed two songs in that roadhouse scene: "Crazy for You" and "Gambler." Both went on to become major hits. In fact, "Crazy for You" garnered Madonna her first Grammy nomination. Ironically, the film was retitled *Crazy for You* for its European release. I guess they wanted to ride the coattails of a hit song and capitalize on Madonna's fame as she'd achieved superstardom with the success of "Crazy for You," which came out between the time we'd shot the movie and the time it hit screens. Geffen Records released a music video of it using the footage from the film.

Jon Peters was a volatile character and could be intimidating. He projected an air of violence that could even intimidate studio heads. I was witness to some of it. He referred to them as knuckleheads. There's a saying, "all men are boys," and when a bully is present, they tend to back off. I don't think it was deliberate on Jon's part. It was just his nature.

Jon certainly was a relief from the cookie cutters. He sometimes referred to me as his "Dylan." I assume he was referring to Bob. I guess I was as much of an enigma to him as he was to me.

While still in preproduction, I got a call from Jon. He was at a photoshoot with some of our actors and had a problem he needed my help with.

When I got there, it was bedlam. Jon had visited the studio where they were doing a fashion shoot. I hadn't felt our presence was needed, but obviously Jon had shown up anyway. He had come in like a bull in a china shop and upset everybody. I was there to get everything back on track, thankful that we were shooting on location where Jon, true to his word, rarely visited.

The only real hiccup in my relationship with Jon was over the music. Well, not exactly the music; we were both in agreement about that. It was about how loud the music was played. In the roadhouse scene, Jon wanted to push it to the point where it drowned out the dialogue. I wasn't doing a music video and wouldn't back down.

Bob Daly, the head of Warner, came in to "arbitrate." Of course, he came down on the side of the producers. Later, when I found out that Jon and Peter owned the music rights, it all made sense. To them, if the scene played like a music video, so much the better.

Vision Quest was technically a sports film, even though I always saw it as a unique coming-of-age drama. That was really at the heart of Davis's novel. It was traditional in Indigenous cultures for a boy to be sent on a "vision quest," a solo journey that would be his initiation into manhood. For Louden Swain, his quest for the high school wrestling championship was his "vision quest."

High school wrestling is an intense, exciting sport, but its audience is relatively small. As Barbra Streisand said after Jon showed her the picture, "Who cares about wrestling?" But Barbra was off the mark. It wasn't just about wrestling, it was about sports in general—one of the few things that brings us together and lifts us up, sometimes in the millions. It is summed up in the inspired speech that Darryl Ponicsan wrote for J. C. Quinn when Louden, played by Matthew Modine, stops by, full of doubt, on the eve of his championship match. The whole film comes down to this moment, and I quote:

> J. C.: You ever hear of Pele?
>
> Matthew: Yeah, he's a soccer player.
>
> J. C.: A very famous one. I was in the room here one day watching a match. I am watching what this guy can do with a ball and his feet. The next thing I know, he jumps up in the air and does a somersault and kicks the ball in upside-down and backwards. The goddamn goalie never knew what hit him. Pele gets excited, takes off his shirt, and starts running around the stadium, waving it over his head. I'm here, sitting alone in my room, crying. That's right, crying. Because another human being, a species that I happen to belong to, can kick a ball and lift himself and the rest of us sad-ass human beings, if only for a minute, to a better place."

Thirty-five years later, I met James Cameron at an Oscar party. He brought up the "Pele" scene. After all that time, it was still fresh in his memory, as it was in mine because it spoke to the power of sports to bring us all together.

When casting *Vision Quest*, I had a talent pool of young actors from *Taps* to choose from, but I was looking for a kid who had "hay in his hair." I found him in newcomer Matthew Modine. For his love interest, I found another newcomer, Linda Fiorentino, fresh off the bus from South Philly, as urban as you can get.

As with *Taps*, a long rehearsal period was required to turn a group of young actors into a championship high school wrestling team. I brought in Cash Stone, a top high school wrestling coach in Spokane, and rehearsals started with a five-mile run.

While the film was well-received, it's true it wasn't football, but it did introduce a young actor of great promise, Matthew Modine, who went on to star in Stanley Kubrick's great war film *Full Metal Jacket* (1987) and Alan Parker's *Birdy* (1984).

Coincidentally, I first saw J. C. Quinn, who speaks those memorable lines about Pele, in *Heartland*, the off-Broadway play that I "discovered" Sean Penn in.

Another actor worth mentioning was my "lucky penny" Ronny Cox, who had played Pierce Brooks, the lead detective in *The Onion Field*, the commanding officer in the confrontation with the cadets in *Taps*, and finally Larry Swain, Louden's father, in *Vision Quest*.

CHAPTER 16
THE BIG TOWN (1987)

"Why would anyone, leery of studio interference, go to Ransohoff, the man who fired Peckinpah off of *The Cincinnati Kid* and took *The Fearless Vampire Killers* away from Polanski."

—Quentin Tarantino

The Big Town, a noir-ish love story about a young crapshooter and a stripper set in the tenderloin of Chicago in the '50s caught my attention.

The producer was Martin Ransohoff, whose reputation preceded him. Everything I'd heard about him screamed stay away. He was a major Hollywood producer whose successes included *The* Sandpiper (1965) with Elizabeth Taylor. It obviously was a big picture for him because he never stopped talking about it.

I had just finished working with Jon Peters, a producer who could rattle the cage; even though it had turned out well, I didn't want to get into a similar situation. I can only compare it to being involved with somebody who can suddenly become violent. It may never manifest itself, but it's always there, lurking in the shadows.

One of my agents at CAA, Marty Baum, also represented Ransohoff and had brought me the project. He assured me it would go well, that I could handle Martin. Famous last words.

Baum arranged a dinner for me and my wife, Susan, and Martin and his wife, Joan. The dinner went well, and most importantly, I really liked Joan. I thought, *How bad can he be with such a nice wife?*

So, in spite of some misgivings, I committed to the film. Things went surprisingly well; the production was pretty much in my hands. Martin was busy with other projects, and he assured me—much as Jon Peters had—that he never went to locations. We were shooting in Toronto for budget reasons, but we had one week in Chicago to set the background for our film. We planned to shoot in the Loop in the seedy part of town to establish the burlesque houses, the bars, and the flophouses where our story took place.

I had put together a cast that I was excited to work with: Matt Dillon, who was just breaking out of his impressive teenage roles; Diane Lane, who I had always wanted to work with; and Tommy Lee Jones, who needs no introduction.

The night before our first day of shooting, we had a sendoff dinner in Chicago with Martin and Joan. Joan was from Chicago, and we dined at the restaurant where she had first met Martin. It added a sentimental touch to our dinner. Martin wished me well; he was on his way back to LA in the morning, and I was starting my shoot.

We were scheduled to film five nights in Chicago, mostly exteriors. We planned to shoot the interiors on studio stages in Toronto. The work went well, things always seemed to move slowly during night shoots. So by Friday night, I knew I had more on my plate than I could complete without going into overtime.

Union rules being what they are, going into overtime on Friday night was costly. After midnight, we automatically went into double time, but there was no alternative. I needed the shots. Our work in Toronto depended on them, and extending into the following week would have cost even more.

We had built the facade of our burlesque theater over an existing theater in the Loop. Matt Dillon exiting the burlesque house was the last shot of the evening. I was still shooting down the street when my production designer came running in to tell me that Martin had ordered the construction crew to start striking the burlesque theater marquee to prevent me from shooting the scene and keep me from going into overtime.

I dropped everything, ran down the street to find the strike crew already dismantling the marquee we had constructed there. I stopped the work and called Martin to explain how much we needed that shot. But before I could finish, the beast was out of its cage, roaring, "You will fucking do what I tell you!" My answer was "That is the last thing you will ever say to me." And it was. I quit the picture.

The next day was a tough one. I wanted to leave it all behind as quickly as possible—the weeks of prep, of casting, of putting together a crew, of finding locations, rehearsals, and a week of shooting. We were on our way. My control of the production had been an illusion. "You will fucking do what I tell you" summed it up.

I said goodbye to Matt and Diane. It was uncomfortable. They were under contract, and the less said, the better. Tom Mack, my assistant director who had been with me on all my films, left with me. Tom's wife was with him, and the three of us wandered around Chicago in a daze, waiting for our flight home. But it wasn't as simple as all that. Yes, I had had breakfast that morning with Diane and Matt. We had spent weeks together—what with the script readings and rehearsals, creating costumes, hair and makeup—and now there was just an uncomfortable silence between us.

The rest of the team—a cinematographer I had taken a chance on, the production designer, costume, hair and makeup—were all on their way to Toronto without missing a beat, without a word spoken. It was a job.

My lawyer, Alan Hergott, was furious with me. "You should have let him fire you, then you would have been paid." My contract had a pay or play clause. Alan was probably right, but in the heat of the moment I knew I couldn't continue to work with Martin. What if he didn't fire me? What then?

David Putnam, the head of Columbia, was a Brit that I had known in London in the '60s when he was hustling for photographers and had wanted to represent me. He was part of the British wave that announced at the Academy Awards that the British were coming. Sure they were—so were the French, the Italians, and the Germans. That's what made American films great. Putnam helped Martin replace me with a novice who was the son of a friend.

My only satisfaction was that the picture opened to the lowest take of any picture in Columbia's history. Two hundred and fifty dollars a theater. Talent is wasted when monsters sit on the throne. I should have listened to my better angels. Bad reputations are usually well-deserved.

I have at times reflected on whether I had overreacted. Backing off was not in my nature. After all, I had a great cast and a film I wanted to make. But I knew deep down that you can't dance with the devil. You're always watching your steps when you do.

After my experience with the five-hundred-pound gorilla, I'd had had it with the studios. I was looking for a project I could control. I wanted to be back in independent filmmaking.

CHAPTER 17
THE BOOST (1988)

I had come across a book I liked, *Ludes* by Benjamin Stein, and felt it had potential as a film. It's a story about drugs, specifically quaalude addiction, but I felt cocaine was a more powerful metaphor.

The main character, Lenny, a modern-day Willy Loman, is out there "with a smile on his face and a shine on his shoes" selling real estate in Los Angeles. It was the '80s, and the market was booming. I immediately thought of Jimmy Woods. I knew he would make a great salesman. We had been in the trenches together, and I thought, *Let's do it again.* I brought in Darryl Ponicsan, who had written *Taps* and *Vision Quest*, to adapt the book, and attached Jimmy to play the lead. I presented this package to John Daly at Hemdale Film Corporation since they made small-budget independent pictures. It was their kind of movie.

The Boost is set against the hedonistic lifestyle of the '80s. Everyone was getting rich, including Lenny, the hard-charging salesman. For Lenny's beautiful wife, Linda, I cast Sean Young, who had made an impression on me in Ridley Scott's unforgettable *Blade Runner* (1982).

One of my favorite lines in *The Boost* is "How did she wind up with a runt like me?" It was straight out of the James Woods playbook. Lenny's cocaine-fueled rise plays itself out in a pivotal scene at one of the Hollywood eateries where the rich and famous had front row seats, the losers relegated to the rear. On any given night, Morton's, a steakhouse that was *the* place to be seen in the '80s, was filled with the who's who of Hollywood holding court at the front tables. It was a long walk to the rear.

To impress his clients, Lenny sets the scene for his "deal of the century" at Morton's, only to have it unravel when the table that he thought he had bribed the maître d' for ends up in the rear among the gawkers and the wannabes. To add insult to injury, I placed Lenny's table near the kitchen doors. Waiters passing to and fro served as a constant reminder of the slight.

His fragile ego crumbling, Lenny descends into a drug-fueled hell, bringing his wife down with him. It was a dark metaphor for the "Roaring '80s."

The last thing you want when doing a love story—albeit a troubled one—is for the actors to actually become personally involved. When Sean brought me the "good news" that she and Jimmy were in love, I was at a loss for words. What was I going to say? "This isn't a good idea," or "Can't you wait until we wrap?" I knew it wouldn't bode well; life isn't the movies. Relationships have their ups and downs. And I knew it would be a tempestuous relationship. We're talking about two volatile actors, one of them married at the time, the other in a long-term relationship. Whatever was happening in their off-screen lives would certainly carry over when they came to the set.

And of course it did. With just a few scenes left to shoot, Jimmy came down with pneumonia and had to be hospitalized. No wonder, considering the strain he was under. We were at our wits' ends keeping Sean from visiting him while his wife was at his bedside. Fortunately, we just had one scene left to shoot with Sean.

It was a night scene, and she arrived with her hair suddenly cut short. I don't know what possessed her to do it. Somehow, I wasn't surprised; it spoke to something in her that was beyond my comprehension. We hurriedly got a wig for her and avoided close ups.

We were shooting at Pink's, a renowned hot dog stand in West Hollywood, and the scene involved Sean eating a hot dog. I was so incensed by Sean's behavior that I did twenty-three takes of her eating that hot dog one bite at a time.

Fortunately, for Jimmy, the acting came first. He was brilliant, and we had enough from Sean to be able to piece together a performance.

In spite of some good notices, the film slipped in and out of the theaters. My feelings about the film were marred by something that happened in postproduction. During the editing process, I found out that John Daly was recutting the picture behind my back. I heard he had a propensity for that kind of egregious behavior. I just didn't think he would do it to me. With the Director's Guild behind me, I stopped it in its tracks, but it soured my relationship with Hemdale and affected the film's release.

Some years later, I crossed paths with Sean Young again when I was invited to the Cognac Film Noir Festival, where my film *Malice* (1993) was in competition. Boarding the charter taking us to Cognac, I noticed Sean on the plane. It turned out, ironically, that not only was she going to the festival, but she was on the jury as well.

I consoled myself with enjoying Cognac—a nice place to spend a few days—only to be surprised by Sean's early exit from the jury and our winning first prize. I guess saner heads had prevailed. Sidney Lumet was the head of the jury.

Years after the release, I received a call from MGM, who had purchased the rights to *The Boost* and were releasing it on DVD. They asked if I would come in to color correct the digital version and add commentary. It was the first time I was seeing the film since finishing it ten years earlier.

It was like seeing it for the first time, and in a sense, it was. I was seeing the film free of all of the distractions that accompanied its initial release. I was so impressed with Jimmy's performance that I asked him to do the commentary with me.

It's not the only time this has happened to me. Years after the release of *Sea of Love* (1989), the Cinematheque in LA showed the film at the Aero Theatre in Santa Monica. While *Sea of Love* had been a hit, this was a richer, more rewarding experience, free of the pressures and expectations of the original release. Al Pacino was in the audience with me and had a similar experience.

For me, it also brought back the first time I met Al on *Johnny Handsome* (1989). Charles "Chuck" Roven, the producer, brought me onto the project.

Johnny Handsome was the ironic name given to the main character by his confederates in the underworld because his appearance was so grotesque. Only the members of his gang would find humor in such a moniker. The film's plot is a well-worn trope. Its roots go back to *The Man in the Iron Mask* (1939), maybe even further back than that. Our hero is betrayed by his fellow gang members and ends up in prison, where he is a perfect candidate for plastic surgery. He emerges from the surgery truly handsome, his name finally befitting him. He is Johnny Handsome, no longer recognizable to those in his former life. The last act, of course, is his revenge on those who betrayed him.

It's a great premise for a crime melodrama, but only if we had an actor capable of convincingly making the transition.

Al Pacino was perfect for the role. He was interested, and we decided to do a make-up test to be sure we could make it work, that the transition would be believable.

We booked a suite at a hotel and brought in a great makeup artist to transform Pacino into the grotesque version of Johnny. After about three hours in makeup, Al walked over to the large mirror above the mantle and stared at himself. I watched as he transformed himself into the character. His head leaned forward, one eye half shut, his back became hunched, his arms grew longer. I wasn't witnessing a transformation—it was more like a transmutation. The image of Al shuffling around that room, trying on his new persona, was unforgettable. Johnny Handsome came alive. It was an amazing experience. Al is truly a shapeshifter.

Unfortunately, we never made the film. Al wanted a new third act, not the predictable revenge story. I agreed with him. It was a B-movie plot, no matter how well we did it. Wouldn't it be great if we could come up with a less predictable ending? Unfortunately, we never did. Al and I often thought of revisiting the project, but we had both moved on. The memory of his transformation stayed with me.

CHAPTER 18
SEA OF LOVE (1989)

I received a call from Tom Pollock, who had been my lawyer before becoming the chairman of Universal. He informed me that I would be getting a call from Martin "Marty" Bregman, who was producing a film called *Sea of Love* starring Al Pacino. The timing couldn't have been better.

I was going home. This was my first New York film. All the people involved in it were New Yorkers, including Marty Bregman, the producer; Richard Price, the writer; and, of course, Al Pacino.

I had always been a fan of Richard Price, who I knew primarily as a novelist. He had a great ear for dialogue, especially New York dialogue and cop dialogue.

Sea of Love is the story of a New York detective, Frank Keller, on the trail of a serial killer, who uses the personal ads to lure in their victims. Our cop, Al Pacino, falls in love with his chief suspect, Helen Cruger, played by Ellen Barkin. It's a love story in the guise of a crime thriller. The focus of the film is the hunt for a serial killer, but the heart of the story, its passion, lies in the relationship of our two main characters. It is the chemistry between Al and Ellen that we are invested in.

Al was perfect for the part. Frank Keller a well-written portrait of a New York cop, lonely and beset by the demons of his trade, who finds the love of his life in his hunt for the killer.

With Ellen, I had the perfect matchup. Al's charisma was contagious. The chemistry was there.

While I knew Al after briefly working with him on *Johnny Handsome*, Marty Bregman was another story. Not only was he the film's producer, but he was also Al's manager. Al and Marty had a deep relationship that went back a couple of decades or so. He had produced some of Al's great films including *Serpico* (1973) and *Dog Day Afternoon* (1975).

I had met Marty in 1971 when I was looking for financing for *After Leaving Mr. Mackenzie*. He represented some major talent, Al being the jewel in his crown. In fact, when meeting with Marty in his office at the time, he was suddenly called away. He excused himself and went into the hall for an unexpected meeting with Al. I couldn't hear much of what was said in their heated conversation, but I surmised that it had something to do with Marty insisting that Al fly to the West Coast. It was only later that I found out it was about Al meeting on *The Godfather*. Later, much later, Marty told me about what he had to go through to get Al onto that plane. But the rest is history.

Marty was a domineering presence, and he quickly made it clear that he was running the show. Fortunately, it was Al who was central. It was his picture. Al and I had lengthy meetings about the script. We had shared concerns. The script had obvious strengths, but we felt it was still a work in progress. For Marty, who viewed himself as the guardian of the script, it was set in stone. I didn't see it that way, and, thankfully, Al didn't either. In the push and pull, Al and I developed a stronger relationship. It was out of that relationship that *Sea of Love* was born.

I vividly remember the first rehearsal. We had assembled a solid cast, and this was the first time we all were together, seated around the table for the first script reading. The excitement was palpable. We were about to embark on a great adventure.

I was at the head of the table, Al to my right, Ellen across from him, the rest of the cast assembled around us, ready to begin when Marty entered the room. I realized that he planned to sit in on the reading. This was a challenging moment for me. There was no way I was going to do the reading with the producer at the table. This was about the director and the actors—a place to be free to express ourselves, to get to know each other. An outsize presence, especially an authority figure like Marty Bregman, did not belong there. It would be like an orchestra with two conductors on the podium.

It was a terrible moment for me. I knew I didn't have the power to ask Marty to leave, but with him at the table, I knew I couldn't proceed. I was about to get up and walk out of the room and out of the picture, when Al leaned in and asked me to ask Mr. B (that's how he referred to Marty) to leave. I was flooded with relief. I felt that Al had saved the picture, or at least the picture I wanted to make.

It was a bumpy ride with Marty after that. I'd call it a ten rounder, but in postproduction, we became friends. It's friendship that has lasted a lifetime.

The driving force, the key to the film, was Frank Keller, a NYPD detective, twenty years on the force and carrying the weight of those years. The only thing that keeps him going is his work, his passion, and his search for a killer at large in the city.

By the first day of shooting, after weeks of rehearsal, Al had become that cop. It didn't surprise me. I had had a taste of it when he had stood in front of a mirror and become Johnny Handsome a couple years earlier. We had a wonderful cast, but Al brought something more. He was a rising tide that lifted all boats. Simply put, he raised everyone's game. There was John Goodman, playing Al's partner Sherman Touhey, and of course, Ellen Barkin, who matched

Al step by step. That was the chemistry that made the film work. It was the heartbeat that drove the story.

Most people reading the script thought the crime story carried the love story. I saw it the other way around. It was the love story that gave it heat—that was its emotional underpinning.

We must have done about fourteen or fifteen takes of the first scene we shot. There are actors I have worked with for whom three or four takes are sufficient, unless they flub a line or miss a cue. After the third or fourth take, it becomes repetitious or, even worse, begins to go downhill. Not with Al. Each take was different, often subtly so. He truly becomes the character he is playing. There's a cliché that it's not about acting, it's about *becoming*. When you become, it rings true. Bo Goldman, a great screenwriter, once told me that when writing dialogue, "If it doesn't jingle, it jangles." This is true of acting as well.

After shooting our first scene, Al called me over and asked me which take I liked. I was taken aback. Was this a test? And would I pass? I answered honestly, and it was a great relief that he agreed. It meant that we were on the same page. Later—it may have even been in postproduction—I came to realize that Al had an uncanny ability to remember the takes that he felt worked. Many times during the shoot, when talking about takes we liked, he might say, "That's good, but take a look at this other one."

We went into the shoot with a major handicap. The Writers Guild had called a strike, and Richard Price was no longer available to us. I had always worked closely with writers from rehearsals through the editing. There was always rewriting to be done. The script was always subject to change depending on so many factors not anticipated at the start of production. From word changes to scenes changes, our script was a work in progress, and we didn't have access to our writer. We couldn't even call Richard at home. The Writers Guild forbade it.

We solved the problem the only way we could. Al and I would often meet after the day's shoot to work on the upcoming scenes. Sometimes we would bring in the other actors and improvise as we rehearsed the scene, making changes as we worked on it. Sometimes it was only a line here or there that gave the scene a lift or turned the corner, but sometimes it was a more radical rewrite. Our script supervisor was with us during these improvisations and would note the changes.

If they were substantial, I would show them to Marty, who was averse to changing anything. We needed to shoot the studio-approved script, no changes—*period*. Al and I didn't see it that way. Everything in a film is in a state of flux, right down to the final cut. There is always the unexpected. Some things just don't work as it may have on the page, and some things surpass your expectations. The key is adapting as you go along.

One morning, we hit the wall. I presented Marty with the amended scene, in this case, the pivotal love scene. We had done significant work, rehearsing, improvising, and finally coming up with the scene we wanted to shoot. I presented it to Marty the morning of the shoot. He was vehement in his rejection. The scene was to be shot as originally scripted and approved by the studio. He felt we had gone too far.

Normally, I had kept Al out of my confrontations with Marty, but I had hit the wall. I went over to Al's trailer. He was in undershorts and a T-shirt when I entered. When I told him what had happened, he burst out of his trailer and announced "This is war" as he marched across the lot in his underwear to Marty's office to confront him. Marty, after a lot of threats about closing down the production, finally backed down.

What made this pivotal scene unique is the emotion Al and Ellen brought to it. It informs what draws these disparate characters together. It's in the foreplay that begins with their serendipitous meeting in the street one evening. From there, it's one long dance to its inevitable conclusion.

Like any dance, we were learning the steps as we created them. Hence the long rehearsals and improvisations. I couldn't have had two more inspired performers than Al and Ellen. Their chemistry was palpable. By the time we had done our work, I knew how to put it on film.

Another scene that has special resonance for me took place in Ellen's upscale shoe salon. Al stops by, and during a flirtatious moment between them, two punks enter the store. They belligerently confront Ellen, and when Al intercedes, the two punks, realizing he is a cop, quickly back off. I'll let Richard Price take it from here.

> Ellen (backing away from Al as though he were contagious): So, you're a cop.
>
> Al: Just too much for you, huh? You let scum in here but my being a cop is just too much. (Holding up his badge) Let me tell you something about all those people in here with their rocks and their furs. They get robbed, they get raped, and all of a sudden, I'm their daddy. Come the wet ass hour, I'M EVERYBODY'S DADDY!"

I was blessed to have Tom Mack as my first assistant. He started with me on *The Onion Field*, and we did eleven films together. He was a pro in the best sense of the term. One day, I was on the set with Tom when Al walked by. Tom turned to me and said, "There goes royalty." This was unusual for Tom, who was rather taciturn and almost never commented on talent. That wasn't his province. Maybe that is why it stayed with me. "There goes royalty."

The first time you *really* see the film is with an audience. Sure, you know the film intimately, but that screening with an audience is a different experience. It gives you some distance from the intense relationship you've had with the film. You're experiencing firsthand what the audience is seeing, when the audience gets it and you should move on, or when they don't and maybe you should take another look.

I'll never forget the first screening of *Sea of Love* for an audience. I knew they were with us. I felt it. I was part of that audience. And then we came to the climactic scene between Al and the killer. After a life and death struggle, Al gets the drop on the killer. And here we did something we thought was an original take on what happens next. The obvious move would be Al taking the killer down, but Richard Price had written a more original ending, and I loved it. The killer, knowing it's over, calmly backs up to the window and jumps out, Al watching impotently. He has the gun, but a gun can't stop a man from killing himself, unless you want to do it for him. This is our climactic moment, and our hero is robbed of it.

Unfortunately, the audience felt robbed as well. I could feel the audience's disappointment. In that moment, we lost them. We chose to reshoot the scene and live up to the audience's expectations. We had promised them a fight to the finish. They had spent two hours with us anticipating it. We couldn't pull the rug out from under them.

The last day of the shoot was also the last scene of the film. It starts with Ellen leaving her shop on Fifty-Seventh Street. It's rush hour, and the street is filled with people hurrying home. Al is waiting for Ellen, but she brushes him off. They've had a serious falling out, and Al is trying to win her back as they push through the crowd.

Normally, we would have surrounded the actors with a crowd of extras we could control. I had asked for two hundred extras to meld into the crowd. This was Fifty-Seventh Street, one of the busiest arteries in the city, at rush hour. Unfortunately, the studio cut the number in half to save money. Shooting on a crowded street filled with people going home from work is fraught with difficulty. Penny-wise and pound-foolish, we were really winging it.

And then it happened. The one thing we couldn't control. Out of nowhere, a heavyset man, obviously in a hurry, barged into our shot and literally banged into Al, knocking him backward. Normally, I'd yell cut, but by this time, I knew Al well enough to keep the cameras rolling. And sure enough, Al bounced back into the shot and kept going without missing a beat. It was New York, and this was an everyday occurrence. It made the final cut and adds credibility to the scene.

And with that, we wrapped. I couldn't wait to get back to LA and into the editing room, finally alone with my film. It had been a great adventure in spite of my difficult relationship with my producer. One moment I was in the street with a crew of fifty to sixty people, and the next, I was alone with my film and my editor.

Again, I had the good fortune to be working with a great editor, David Bretherton. His brilliant work on *Cabaret* (1972), an editing tour de force, more than qualified him. David had been with me throughout the shoot and was already putting scenes together. But now the real work began.

His background as a musician served him well. He had a feel for the rhythm, the pace that drives a film.

I had yet another reason to look forward to getting back. I felt that the studio would have my back in my dealings with Marty.

***

No sooner did we have our feet on the ground than we were in conflict over the choice of a composer. Now, in my experience, this was a director's prerogative. Of course, Marty didn't see it that way.

Tom Pollock had been a major entertainment lawyer before moving to Universal. Since he had been my lawyer, I viewed him as a friend. It was why I was happy to be back at the studio. I asked for his support in dealing with the choice of composers, only to be told that he thought that adversity was great for the "creative process." There certainly had been plenty of that.

In my naivety, it didn't dawn on me that Tom might have had an even closer relationship with Marty. I realized I was on my own and had to make peace with Marty. I was seeing a therapist at the time, and she told me that in order to diffuse the situation, I had to "white light" Marty. Yes, those are the words she used. I had to go the distance. I had to put aside any thought of confrontation and embrace Marty. Yes, literally *embrace* him. We met in his office, and as I walked around his desk, he pulled back and rose. Thinking he was in harm's way, he grabbed his cane. Instead, I embraced him. It totally disarmed him. I had gone halfway, more than halfway, and he responded in kind. From that moment, we were in it together.

As to choosing a composer, I had seen Alan Parker's *Mississippi Burning*, and the score by Trevor Jones had impressed me. It felt more like an effects track. It had a drive to it without being melodic. I had a "melody," it was the title of my film and the background to the murder that opens it. And when we hear it again in the film, it evokes the memory of that murder and becomes a very effective cue. I didn't want a score that competed with that cue, In fact, when *Sea of Love* was released in France, they retitled it *Mélodie Pour un Muerte* ("Melody for a Murder").

Trevor gave us a brilliant score that spoke to the suspense and darkness at the heart of our story. Still, I was looking for something romantic to play against it. I was looking for Al's theme. Something lonely and haunting. My inspiration was Miles Davis's score for *Elevator to the Gallows* (1958) as it accompanies Jeanne Moreau through the dark streets of Paris. We found what we were looking for in a brilliant saxophonist whose improvisation begins under the opening credits and sets the tone for the film.

Choosing a composer is critical. So much rides on it. There's no script for the score. It's uncharted territory. Of course, the composer has the film to inform them. You give them that, and you try to convey what you're looking for, but you're not a musician. You can't sit down at the piano and speak to them in their language, and you don't want to hem them in with specific references.

Usually, the composer sketches out the themes for the score on the piano. This is the first time you get an idea of what to expect and have a chance to react to it, but it's only with a full orchestra at the recording studio that you really hear the score. By that time, it's too late to make any significant changes. Years later, when I worked with Jerry Goldsmith on *Malice*, our first film together, computer technology made it possible for me to hear a reasonable facsimile of how the score would sound with a full orchestra.

On my first recording session for *The Ragman's Daughter*, I was in awe of being in the presence of the members of the London Philharmonic playing our score. But I noticed that between takes, they would read magazines and newspapers, yet when the baton came down, they would play the notes without missing a beat. For me, it was magic. For them, it was a job.

Music is the fourth dimension of a film, especially in the hands of a gifted composer like Jerry Goldsmith, whose iconic scores included *Patton*, *Chinatown* (1974), and countless other films including *Malice* and *City Hall*, the two films he scored for me.

While working on *Malice*, I happened to hear a broadcast of a children's choir. The voices had a purity and innocence that I thought would be the perfect introduction to *Malice*, which takes place in an all-girls college. Jerry loved the idea and took it from there, incorporating it into his score.

Malice opens on images of a bucolic campus, a choir of virginal voices filling the air. Marrying Gordon Willis's images with Jerry's score plays like an overture to an innocence that will soon be upended.

A haunting saxophone solo draws us into the world of *Sea of Love*, which opens with long tracking shots of the city at night. Much as I had in my short film *Blind Gary Davis,* I used a Volkswagen bus as a moving platform, trolling the city.

Late in the evening, we ended up at the entrance to the Lincoln Tunnel, which was alive with hookers working the line of trucks waiting to enter the tunnel.

One girl, completely nude except for a transparent raincoat, was running from truck to truck, plying her trade, and she became one of the images in our title montage.

Now normally when shooting alfresco, production teams would have a follow car getting signed releases from the people we filmed. Unfortunately, we were doing the title on a shoestring budget that didn't include a follow car. After the film's release, I received a call from Universal's legal department; the girl in the transparent coat was suing us for harming her reputation. Universal offered to settle for twenty-five thousand dollars, but on the bad advice of her lawyer, she insisted on going to court where the judge ruled against her, saying her reputation was not an issue.

CHAPTER 19
MALICE (1993)

I have always felt a certain kinship with cinematographers, and they have often become personal friends. In some ways, we are cut from the same cloth. We come from the same world, going all the way back to my days as a photographer. I understand how key they are. Great cinematographers like Michael Seresin, who I made several films with, starting with *The Ragman's Daughter*, and Charles "Chuck" Rosher Jr., who was the cinematographer for *The Onion Field*, bring so much to a film. His father was Charles Rosher Sr., who won the first Academy Award for Best Cinematography in 1928 for the classic film *Sunrise* (1927) from the great German director F. W. Murnau.

Chuck grew up in Hollywood and would regale me with stories of early Hollywood. His father had worked with Charlie Chaplin, Douglas Fairbanks, and Mary Pickford. I was even more interested in his recollections about Murnau, who had made *Nosferatu* (1922), one of my favorite silent films.

And then there was Owen Roizman. We did three films together, starting with *The Black Marble*. I feasted on his stories of working with Billy Friedkin, who blew everyone away with *The French Connection* and *The Exorcist*, two films photographed by Owen that couldn't have been more different in style. Thirty years later, at a dinner party given by his wife, Sherry Lansing, Billy Friedkin toasted me for *The Onion Field*. The circle closed. I was not only working with great cinematographers, I was learning from them.

Cinematographers create the images that are the unique signature of the film. Think of *Citizen Kane* (1941). From its first frame, you are in the hands of a master, Gregg Toland. Toland shot Kane's scenes in the newsroom from extremely low angles, giving Kane a larger-than-life presence. In contrast, there's the hushed tones of the library where the search for Kane begins, viewed in a smoke-filled haze that the hard light of the projector showing newsreels of Kane's life cuts through.

In *Last Tango in Paris* (1972), Vittorio Storaro, a more contemporary master, manipulated the temperature of the lights to bathe Marlon Brando and Maria Schneider in a warm, romantic glow juxtaposing the cold light of the exteriors.

And there I was, working with their contemporaries.

I did *Malice* with Gordon "Gordie" Willis, who holds a special place in the pantheon. His work on *The Godfather* alone should earn him a place among the immortals.

Each film brings its own challenges. It may be a producer who metamorphizes into a monster or an actor who, early in the film, requests a few days off later in the shoot to get married.

The actor was Alec Baldwin, a great but volatile talent. The bride-to-be was Kim Basinger. I agreed it wouldn't be a problem. The time off he was asking for was far enough in the future that we could easily schedule around his absence. As we got closer to that day, however, it wasn't as easy as I had hoped.

We had a key scene between Nicole Kidman and Alec at a secluded beach house. After much searching, we found the ideal location. Critically, it was close enough so that we could make it a one-day shoot including travel. There was only one rub—it was a wet beach. This is a beach that, because of the tides, is above water for a limited time. We needed access to the beach for a few hours, and it just so happened that there were only a few days that the tides were right and the beach would be dry for the few hours we required to film the scene. Coincidentally, those were the days Alec had asked to take off to get married.

I had the unfortunate task of informing Alec that we couldn't give him the time off. I dreaded the confrontation, as I was already aware of his temper. There was a moment when after delivering the bad news, I didn't help matters by adding, "We're making a movie, Alec," as though that trumped everything.

I saw the color rising in Alec's face and prepared for the worst. In a rage, Alec burst out of my trailer and into producer Charles "Chuck" Mulvehill's trailer.

Chuck bore the brunt of Alec's anger. I think I actually saw Chuck's trailer shaking. Thankfully, it wasn't me. The story had a happy ending, though I didn't learn of it until having dinner with Alec in New York a couple of years later. He told me that on their anniversary, he and Kim would toast me for forcing them to postpone their wedding until the beginning of the following year. Kim had been sued for breach of contract for pulling out of a film, and she had lost the suit and all of her money. If she and Alec had been married at the time, he would have been liable as well.

Malice (1993)

Malice is the story of a brilliant surgeon named Jed Hill (Alec Baldwin), who conspires with his lover (Nicole Kidman) to commit insurance fraud with unanticipated but deadly consequences. The screenplay, the work of the gifted Aaron Sorkin, is filled with memorable lines. One of my favorites—and certainly the favorite of many doctors—is when at a medical inquiry, while under questioning, Alec (as Dr. Hill) responds:

> Hill: The question is, "Do I have 'God complex'?
>
> Dennis Riley (the questioning attorney): Dr. Kessler says "yes."
>
> Hill: Which makes me wonder if this lawyer has any idea as to the kind of grades one has to receive in college to be accepted at a top medical school. Or if you have the vaguest clue as to how talented someone has to be to lead a surgical team. I have an MD from Harvard. I am board certified in cardiothoracic medicine and trauma surgery. I have been awarded citations from seven different medical boards in New England, and I am never, ever sick at sea. So I ask you, when someone goes into that chapel and they fall on their knees and they pray to God that their wife doesn't miscarry, or that their daughter doesn't bleed to death, or that their mother doesn't suffer acute neural trauma from postoperative shock, who do you think they're praying to? Now, go ahead and read your Bible, Dennis, and you go to your church, and with any luck you might win the annual raffle. But if you're looking for God, he was in operating room number two on November seventeenth, and

> he doesn't like to be second guessed. The question is, do I have a God complex? Let me tell you something: *I am God.*"

Seated around the table for that memorable moment, I was graced with the presence of George C. Scott and Peter Gallagher playing the medical supervisor and the district attorney respectively. It was great to be working with George again a decade after *Taps*.

I was fortunate to have such major talent, if only for one scene, albeit an important one. Good actors have a special presence that helps to quickly define their characters.

Malice was a pure thriller. As we hunt for a serial killer, the true plot unfolds in its shadow. It was an interesting challenge, a little like constructing a clock. All the pieces had to fit to make it tick. As I mentioned, I had the good fortune of having Aaron Sorkin, whose dialogue energized every scene. I cast Nicole Kidman as the femme fatale, Alec Baldwin as the malevolent doctor, and Bill Pullman as the hapless husband.

François Truffaut once described a film as a journey. *Malice* was more of a thrill ride with unexpected twists and turns. And to top it off, I was working with one of the great cinematographers, Gordie Willis. He often called me late at night; he was already thinking about the next day's work. It was the content of the scene that would inform his approach to the framing and lighting. He had a favorite phrase: "Too much wood piling up at the fire door."

Gordie wasn't just a cinematographer, he was also a filmmaker who had a very strong presence on set. He brought a great crew with him. All great cinematographers have great crews that work with them over the years, and they develop a well-oiled machine. Another cinematographer once stopped by and commented on how quiet the set was. It was a sign of the respect that the crew had for Gordie and his intense focus.

Anne Bancroft has only one scene in *Malice*, playing Nicole's mother. I couldn't believe my luck in getting her for this small but pivotal role. When we first met, she informed me that she had never played cards, but by the time we got to her scene seven weeks later, you would have never known it. Within the opening moments of the scene with her son-in-law, played by Bill Pullman, she establishes herself as a card player. You would have thought she stepped out of a casino.

Through the lexicon of a professional card player, she shuffles the deck and offers it to him, "Pick a card." As she lures him in, she lays out the plot for her son-in-law, who is an unwitting part of it.

The exposition pivotal to explaining the plot could have been a long, windy scene, but it is masked by Aaron Sorkin's high-voltage dialogue.

Malice was the kind of film that was constructed like a set of Russian dolls: each scene a stand-alone leading to the next one until the final denouement.

Malice was based on a true story about medical insurance fraud. The challenge was to make a story about fraud, which is usually a white-collar crime, into a compelling, suspenseful drama. The key was to have the underlying greed that motivates the fraud spiral its characters into something much darker.

Faced with the reality forced on him by Anne unmasking her daughter, Bill goes from the hapless husband to a player in our drama. In his subsequent confrontation with Nicole in a restaurant, her true nature reveals itself. When confronted, she explodes in rage, shattering the wineglass she is holding in her hand. At that instant, we realize she is capable of anything—even murder.

There are images unique to film where it all comes together in a memorable moment. For *Malice*, it was the glass shattering in Nicole's hand. It went beyond words, right to the character's ruthlessness and rage.

The black spider crawling down the wall towards the body of Rachel Roberts in Lindsay Anderson's *The Sporting Life* (1963). Richard Harris, in pent up anger, smashing the spider with his fist.

The British officer with his riding crop, pushing the "thirty pieces of silver" to Victor McLaglen, the informer, "filthy money for a filthy deed" in John Ford's *The Informer* (1935).

William Holden at the end of his rope after escaping from the Japanese prison camp, hallucinating and seeing vultures circling over him, only to have them turn into kites flown by village boys who are his salvation in David Lean's *The Bridge on the River Kwai.*

The cat walking down the dark street in Vienna and finding Orson Welles hiding in the doorway in Carol Reed's *The Third Man* (1949).

The language of film.

A language I first became aware of when seeing Sergei Eisenstein's masterpiece *Battleship Potemkin* (1925) at the Irving Place Theatre when I was still in art school. Irving Place was one of the small group of theaters showing foreign films at the time.

Battleship Potemkin was pure cinema. The montage of the slaughter of the innocents on the Odessa Steps is unforgettable: The baby carriage careening down the steps intercut with images of a bereaved mother. The line of soldiers mercilessly marching down the steps, firing at them. It's a sequence of images with an emotional effect far greater than the sum of its parts. This scene is Eisenstein's masterclass in montage.

As I write this, Odessa, a city my mother emigrated from at the age of five in 1906, is again under attack by yet another tyrant.

CHAPTER 20
CITY HALL (1996)

It all started with a parking meter scandal—a very New York story involving corruption in high places and the mafia. It was on Mayor Ed Koch's watch, and Kenneth Lipper, who brought me *City Hall*, had been a deputy mayor in his administration. He knew firsthand where all the bodies were buried.

The borough president of Queens, Donald Manes, was under indictment, as was his partner in crime, Stanley Friedman, head of the Bronx Democratic Party. The two were in league with the mafia, stealing millions from the city in a parking meter scam. Manes committed suicide just an hour after the feds, who had him under surveillance, saw two mafiosos leave his house. Friedman went to jail, serving hard time in a federal prison. Rudy Giuliani had been the federal prosecutor.

Giuliani had been the mayor of New York when Bo Goldman and I were doing our research for *City Hall*. It's hard to square that hard-driving mayor so filled with rectitude to the man who, as I write this in 2023, has been indicted for fraudulently trying to overturn a presidential election. Seeing Giuliani's infamous press conference where hair dye is running down his face reminded me of the great scene in *Death in Venice*—Dirk Bogarde in his dying moment, the hair dye running down his face. Life imitates art.

Ken Lipper and his partner, Edward Pressman, an established independent film producer, brought me the script, which was authored by two distinguished screenwriters, Paul Schrader and Nicholas Pileggi. While I liked the script, I felt it didn't fulfill the potential I saw in the material. This was a big story with many intricate strands.

I had just made *Malice* for Castle Rock, a boutique production company. We worked well together. They were a director-oriented company. One of their principals was Rob Reiner, whose films they produced. With their backing, I approached Bo Goldman to write a new screenplay for *City Hall*.

To me, Bo was the gold standard. His screenplays were always about people, about relationships. He had won two Academy Awards, one for *One Flew Over the Cuckoo's Nest* (1975) and another for *Melvin and Howard* (1980). He was also a born and bred New Yorker. He loved the material, and we set off on our long journey together.

With Ken's connections, we did our own research before setting pen to paper. Ken opened the door for us, and we were able to meet many of the players in the real-life drama. I remember meeting Friedman, who was managing a small hotel on Staten Island after serving four years in maximum security. He had refused to name names and, obviously, those he had protected took care of him.

He arrived for our breakfast meeting at the Regency Hotel in a Cadillac convertible. The Regency was famous for its power breakfasts, where New York's movers and shakers would meet. In those days, as he pointed out, there would be a line of powerbrokers stopping by. Now, we might as well have been in Siberia.

Friedman was tough. He had been a cabdriver, a street guy who had risen to be the head of the Bronx Democratic Party. The feds threw everything they could at him. The mafia knew Friedman could do the time standing on his head. Unfortunately, they didn't have the same confidence in Manes, and after a visit from some mafia capos, he took his own life. It made for a powerful scene in *City Hall*.

We first heard the line, "There's black and there's white, but the gray in between is where we live," from Friedman. It ended up in the mayor's final soliloquy. Most of the players involved in the parking meter scandal were still around. Some, like Friedman, would speak with us. Others would not.

City Hall in lower Manhattan is home to the mayor's office and the city council. While we were able to interview Mayor Giuliani in his office, we couldn't get permission to shoot there and had to build a facsimile for those scenes. We had more luck on the other side of the aisle. The city council allowed us to shoot in their chambers, a valuable asset in an all-location shoot. In fact, the opening scene of *City Hall* was shot in their assembly hall. It has an authenticity that anchors the film.

In casting, my first thought for the mayor was Al Pacino. Charismatic and dynamic, I think if Al actually ran for mayor of New York, he would have been a contender.

Unfortunately, Al was not available. He was committed to an Oliver Stone biopic about Manuel Noriega, the Panamanian dictator. My other choice was Dustin Hoffman, who I also thought was a natural, more in the mold of Ed Koch, who had been the mayor of New York in the '80s. I had first seen Dustin in *Eh?* at the Circle in the Square Theater in Greenwich Village in 1966.

It was theater in the round, and as Dustin made an unforgettable entrance walking in, his body tilted to one side, seeming to defy the laws of gravity. I'll never forget it. He was on his way. Mike Nichols saw him in *Eh?* and cast him in *The Graduate* (1967).

I met Dustin in the late '80s, and we spent time looking for a film to do together. I sent him the script for *City Hall*, and he returned it with six pages of single-spaced notes. Simply put, to even address half of them would have involved a page one rewrite of Bo's script. Changes are always a part of the creative process, but we weren't going to reinvent the wheel. We liked what we had! Dustin was off to the South Seas on a holiday. I called Martin Schafer, the head of Castle Rock, and sent him Dustin's pages. His response was "Let's move on."

Then good fortune smiled on us. The Noriega project had fallen through, and Al became available.

Dustin, on his return from his travels, insisted that we had committed to him and sued us and his agents at CAA. His high-powered lawyer, Bert Fields, had been heard to say, "I can't wait to get Becker on the stand." It put a chill through me.

Ironically, CAA represented Dustin and Al, aside from representing me. Obviously, they wouldn't have made the deal for Al if they had already made one for Dustin. It never went to court. Bert and Dustin reached a settlement with the studio and agency. They walked away with a large sum of money. When I questioned the settlement—after all, I thought we had an ironclad case—the answer was simple: it was cheaper than the cost of litigation.

A minor distraction, but we were on our way with Al as the mayor of New York.

While *City Hall* created its own tale of corruption in high places, it found its inspiration in the months we spent meeting with the people who, in one way or another, had played a part in the parking meter scandal. Bo took it from there.

The death of a young boy, accidentally killed in the opening scene, ultimately brings down a mayor.

I cast Danny Aiello to play Frank Anselmo, a corrupt assemblyman from Brooklyn. I cast him for his charisma and congeniality. His warmth was contagious. His outgoing personality could easily mask the corrupt nature of the councilman he was playing. His love for musicals plays out in a scene of him at the theater enjoying a performance of *Carousel.* He is called away during the performance for a tête-à-tête with the mayor in the theater's lounge. In the ensuing scene, we are treated to a masterclass in political maneuvering between the councilman and the mayor, with *Carousel* playing in the background. It makes his fall that much more heartbreaking.

In Danny's final confrontation with Tony Franciosa (playing mob boss Paul Zapatti), he is no match for the mafia don, for whom sentimentality is an indulgence.

I was fortunate to have Tony Franciosa for the part. I remembered him for his performances in films like *A Hatful of Rain* (1957). He was part of a new generation of leading men who broke the mold, and here he was, an elder statesman both in Hollywood and in my film as the mafia don.

We shot the final confrontation between the councilman and the don on the outside porch of a house in Brooklyn. The location had its challenges. The scene took place on a wide porch surrounding the back and side of the councilman's house. Unfortunately, it looked out on neighboring homes, which, considering the tragic nature of the scene, were a distraction. We solved the problem by secluding the porch, hanging bamboo blinds that my cinematographer, Michael Seresin, pushed the light through to create a more intimate setting.

The scene starts with Danny putting a canary that he loves back in its cage. He kisses it on its little head as he whispers words of endearment. I don't remember how the bird got into the scene, but I think it was serendipity, a prop the set dresser had placed there that I took advantage of, because what follows is the entrance of the don to tell the councilman that it's over.

> Zapatti: I tried to close the door, Frank. Couldn't get it shut.
>
> Anselmo: Well, what do you want me to do?
>
> Zapatti: Take the pressure off yourself... Here's the thing. They'll tell you, "Yeah, yeah, sure you have the key to your cell. Go ahead. But you won't be able to open it without singing. You're a singer, Frank.
>
> Anselmo: Give me a chance, and I-I-I'll show you how quiet I can be.

> Zapatti: It's out of my hands, Frank. Do the right thing, will you? Make it easy for yourself.... And your family.

In the background, we hear the bird chirping. The bird was not scripted, he simply improvised.

Martin Landau, who I was fortunate enough to have cast as the judge, was another major talent who has had a memorable career. Coincidentally, I learned that we had both studied art at Pratt at the same time. Our paths had taken different directions, and we finally met on *City Hall.*

Judge Walter Stern signs the fateful probation report that puts a killer on the streets and seals the fate of a cop and an innocent boy.

When confronted, he falls upon his sword.

> Judge Stern: I knew that when that bullet hit that boy, it would keep traveling...
>
> Calhoun: And find its way...?
>
> Judge Stern: To me. If only it had found me first. If only I could have stepped in front of him. Regrets are pathetic, aren't they? I was tired of being the white shoe litigator.... All it took was fifty thousand dollars to change my life. Fifty thousand and the judgeship was mine. Absurd, isn't it?

It was only a few years since Pacino had played the romantic lead in *Sea of Love*, and there he was as the mayor of New York, looking decades older, delivering a eulogy for a slain child. Only the close-up of Al that follows, so unique to film, could go beyond words to convey the weight of that moment.

Bo's script had that weight. There were speeches, long speeches, the kind of speeches a mayor might make at a funeral oration for a slain child before a hostile congregation of Black churchgoers that he wishes to embrace.

The scene is followed by a close-up of Al in the car carrying him and his deputy away from the funeral. The silence that surrounds him in the close-up is as powerful as the oration it follows. The loss of a child hangs heavy in the air.

In doing our research, we had spent a lot of time with Mayor Giuliani. Being mayor of a metropolis like New York is a hands-on job. I don't know if there's any other like it. The mayor is always rushing from one event to another, whether it's a ribbon cutting or a four-alarm fire. And they're accompanied by an entourage of cars speeding from one location to another: the lead car, the follow cars, the motorcycles clearing the way, and the mayor at its center.

In *City Hall*, the child's death in the first scene brings down the mayor in the final scene. Kevin Calhoun, the deputy mayor played by John Cusack, has idolized the mayor as a paragon of virtue. But when Kevin confronts his mentor in the end, in a final denouement, Mayor Pappas responds:

> Mayor: You want an answer? Okay, Pappy. Think of it as colors. There's black, and there's white. And in between is mostly gray. That's us. Now, gray is a tough color because it's not as simple as black and white. And for the media, certainly not as interesting. But it's who we are....
>
> I had the fire in the belly, just like you Kevin, and the odd thing is, I still have it. It never left me. I had the dream, and I had the weight. Like one of those guys before me said, "If a sparrow dies in Central Park, I feel responsible." Well said; I feel that way. And I was gonna take that feeling with me all the way to Washington.
>
> Kevin: The things you could have done.
>
> Mayor: The things I could have done.

With those final words, the curtain comes down on our drama.

Bo's script and our casting captured the diversity that characterizes New York. Al Pacino as the mayor, a New Yorker to the core; John Cusack, his deputy mayor, a transplant from Louisiana; Bridget Fonda, the feisty Irish lawyer from Queens; Danny Aiello as the councilman from Brooklyn; Tony Franciosa as the mafia don, David Paymer as Abe Goodman, the DA who knows what's "kosher"; and Richard Shiff as the probation officer who knows too much. All distinct voices unique to New York.

When it came to writing credits, there were four listed. Only one of them, Bo Goldman, actually wrote the screenplay. As I had mentioned, two of the other writers, Paul Schrader and Nicholas Pileggi had written a script before I had become involved. When I hired Bo, it was a fresh start. I never even showed him the first script. Kenneth Lipper, who might have at least deserved a story credit, somehow pushed himself in as a "writer." It may not be fair, but the Writers Guild, the final arbiter of writing credits, has a unique arbitration procedure where everyone who thinks they deserve a credit submits their version of the script. Lipper, in his desire for undeserved credit, had hired a top Hollywood lawyer to support his claim. Since I was there and knew who did what, I asked them to allow me to testify as to the authorship. Unbelievable as it may seem, they refused to allow me to speak, hence four writing credits on a script written by one writer, Bo Goldman. The words are his.

Jerry Goldsmith's score filled in the rest. He captured the heartbeat of the city. I was thinking Gershwin; he gave me that and more.

CHAPTER 21
MERCURY RISING (1998)

I first met Brian Grazer in the '80s. He would often stop by my offices at Warner Bros. He was young, full of drive, and on his way. He and his partner, Ron Howard, had a hit film with *Splash* (1984), but Brian had a dilemma. He had made a deal with Warner prior to *Splash* and wanted to renegotiate his deal with the studio. He felt uncomfortable about reopening a deal he had just made. I suggested that he just inform them that the deal he had made "no longer represented his present circumstances." Brian was so pleased with the phrase that he still reminds me of it to this day.

Some fourteen years after our first meeting, he offered me a film to direct called *Mercury Rising*. Actually, the original title was *Mercury Falling*, which was more appropriate since it is the name of a classified code that fails, but the head of the studio didn't want a title that had "falling" in it.

Mercury Rising is a thriller, and at its center is an autistic boy who unwittingly breaks a highly-classified code with major consequences. The boy becomes a threat to national security. His breaking of the code endangers his life, and Bruce Willis, playing a rogue FBI agent, saves the boy's life and becomes his protector.

Bruce was well cast. His work in action movies had made him a star, but he had the chops to play a much more nuanced character. I remember first seeing him in *Moonlighting*, long before he made his name in action films like *Die Hard* (1988).

Normally, a story about a boy in trouble with his life at stake and the man who saves him is emotionally a given. How can you miss? I thought of the scene in *The Kid* where Charlie Chaplin and the kid, Jackie Coogan, are being forcibly separated by the police as they desperately cling to each other. It breaks your heart.

But when the boy is autistic, they may have trouble expressing that kind of feeling. An neurodivergent person does not make emotional connections in the same way a neurotypical person does.

After much research, including spending time at schools for autistic children as well as with their families, I realized the challenge that lay ahead. Autism spectrum disorder (ASD) impairs the ability to communicate and interact. In a story about the relationship between the boy and the world around him, the challenge can be daunting.

I brought in an ASD specialist from the University of Chicago, Dr. Leventhal, to help guide me and the young actor I had cast.

I had seen the emotional toll it took when meeting parents of autistic children. They loved their children, but were never sure if that love was reciprocated. It was heartbreaking.

The challenge for our film was figuring out how to establish a bond between the boy and his protector.

I had never met Bruce prior to being offered *Mercury Rising*, so I arranged to meet with Bruce at his home. Since I had already cast nine-year-old Miko Hughes to play the autistic child, I thought it was important for him to meet Bruce as well. If Bruce had any reservations, that would have been the time to air them.

So I brought Miko with me. It was a cordial meeting, but Bruce seemed somewhat removed. He made no effort to connect with Miko. I thought it strange, but I attributed it to the awkwardness that is always a part of first meetings.

Bruce put me at ease when, to my surprise, he let me know that our paths had crossed through Linda Fiorentino, who I had cast in *Vision Quest*. Bruce explained that he had been a bartender at Cafe Central in Manhattan, a hangout for actors. He was a young actor still knocking on doors, when Linda, who had just arrived in New York, got a job there as a waitress. Bruce had taken her under his wing. Within a few months, she had landed *Vision Quest*, and he was still knocking on doors. As he described it, he would frequently be using the public telephone booth outside the restaurant to call his agent, and there was Linda, just three months in New York and off and running with a lead in a film.

The meeting with Bruce went well, but still there was a feeling of him holding court. It wasn't only the kid who was being auditioned. Who knows, maybe Bruce thought he was being auditioned as well. The coolness I felt that evening foreshadowed our relationship on the film. There was Bruce, and then there were the rest of us. On the one hand, you got through to him, he was a pro and hit his marks. He was brilliant at times, but there was a coldness at the heart of it.

Still, the dynamics of the thriller were well served, but the emotions, the subtext, and the connection with the boy never really took hold. Maybe it was asking too much. Miko was a very good actor and stayed in character. I could have fudged it, but it would have been fake. In fact, I had Dr. Leventhal on the set to guide us.

Autism can a terrible affliction and I didn't want to break away from that. But it simply doesn't make for happy endings.

Bruce is a star. One of the chosen ones. It's not that he can jump higher or that he can run faster—it's about charisma. Only a few are blessed by it, and the camera finds them. We pour our own fantasies into them.

The terrifying moment in *Mercury Rising* when Bruce, as Agent Art Jeffries, saves Miko, as Simon Lynch, from the path of an oncoming train had its genesis in something that had happened to me as a teenager.

I had hitchhiked to Washington, DC, with a friend. We had good luck getting there, but our luck ran out going home. So there we were, in the middle of the night, stranded in some place outside of Philadelphia, only halfway home. We decided to split up to improve our chances of getting a ride. I was alone in the dark, the only light coming from passing cars as they sped down the highway. Suddenly, from out of nowhere, I was caught in the blinding headlights of a train rushing out of the darkness towards me. In a terrifying moment, it hurtled past me, the ground shaking under me.

Unknown to me, there were tracks running parallel to the highway, and the train had appeared and disappeared no more than twenty feet from where I'd stood.

The memory of that terrifying moment all came back to me in creating the scene of Bruce at the side of the road, hiding from the headlights of the passing traffic. He hears the sound of an approaching train and turns to see Miko, the boy he's been protecting, attracted by the headlights of the oncoming train and walking down the tracks towards it. In an explosive moment, Bruce is up and running, snatching the boy from the train's path and tumbling to the other side as the train passes.

Of course, neither cast nor crew were ever in proximity to a moving train. It was all done through the magic of film with the assistance of George Lucas's Industrial Light & Magic (ILM). And Bruce brought his own magic.

Mercury Rising was mostly filmed on location in Chicago, which had plenty of train tracks running parallel to the highways. As a matter of fact, all of my films have been shot on location, from *The Ragman's Daughter* on the streets of Nottingham to *The Onion Field* on the streets of LA. Even working for the studios, I rarely used their stages or backlots. The settings were dictated by the scripts, and the artifice of shooting in a studio was hardly ever an option.

Locations provide an infinite number of possibilities—and challenges. The location adds another dimension that gives depth to the storytelling. For *The Onion Field*, shooting on Carlos and Gower in Hollywood where the police officers were actually kidnapped affected all of us, especially the actors. But shooting on location could be a logistical nightmare, especially in urban settings. Everything had to be mobile, from equipment trucks to cast and crew trailers. With each film, it seemed the number of vehicles I needed to move from one location to another seemed to increase. I went from a single minivan for *The Ragman's Daughter* to one trailer home for *The Onion Field*, which Joe Wambaugh and I shared, to a trailer home for each lead in *Sea of Love*. Of course, it makes sense for Al or Ellen or any other lead to have a personal trailer. Not only for their costumes, hair, makeup, and so on, but more importantly for their privacy.

Actors spend so much time waiting to go on. Their trailer is a sort of refuge for them. When they are on location, they spend a lot of time there.

Trailers and such were not usually my concern. Other people handled those matters. It's taken for granted and comes with the territory. It only concerned me when trailers were far from the set because working on crowded city streets often didn't allow for trailers to have proximity to the location. This became very evident on *Mercury Rising* when Bruce's trailers were stationed ten blocks from the set. This *did* involve me because of the time involved with shuttling Bruce to the set or traveling to meet with him.

Upon inquiring, I learned that the closest parking lot that could accommodate Bruce's four trailers—yes, that's how many trailers his contract called for—was ten blocks away.

Why four trailers? One for Bruce personally; another for his gym; a third for costumes, hair, and makeup; and I forget what the fourth was for. I couldn't help thinking back to my first short film where a VW minivan took me and my crew of four to an apartment in Harlem to shoot *Blind Gary Davis*.

We had completed most of our shooting for *Mercury Rising* in Chicago and were back in LA shooting some interiors on the Universal lot.

While setting up a shot, I noticed Bruce being interviewed on the other side of the set. It must have been an important interview because Brian Grazer, who rarely came to set, had joined them.

Brian introduced me to the interviewer, Bernard Weinraub, a Hollywood reporter for *The New York Times*. He had been a foreign correspondent before show business became his beat. A strange transition, going from covering foreign posts to the gossip columns, but he was married to Amy Pascal, who was the head of a major studio. I assume it gave him a leg up in covering Hollywood.

The first thing Bernie asked me was, "Who is your rabbi?" I was taken aback. Did he think I needed a rabbi to get this job? I had just spent fifteen weeks working with Bruce Willis. Maybe I needed a therapist, but I certainly didn't need a rabbi.

There is an unfathomable chemistry in the relationship between actors and directors. It's simply there or it isn't. With Jimmy Woods, Al Pacino, and a myriad of other actors I worked with, it was there from the start. We were connected, brought together by the work. With Bruce, there was a distance I couldn't bridge. Of course he did his job, and he was good at it. Perhaps it was just stardom that set him apart.

In ancient Rome, when Caesar would lead a victory parade in his chariot on his return from a successful campaign, he would have a slave accompanying him in his chariot to remind him that he was not a god. As Ceasar led the parade of his legions and the spoils of war that Rome feasted on, the slave would continuously whisper to him, "You're only a man."

CHAPTER 22
HAPPY ENDINGS

On the subject of happy endings, I'm reminded of the ending that Richard Price had originally written for *Sea of Love*. After Al Pacino (as Detective Frank Keller) vanquishes the killer, we cut to a small bedroom at night, a young child in a crib. A shadowy figure enters through the window, pauses over the crib, looks down at the sleeping child, then moves stealthily into the adjoining bedroom where Al is asleep. The intruder hovers over Al then grabs him by the throat, strangling him. Suddenly, Al wakes up. We find him in bed with Ellen Barkin (as Helen Cruger). It's a recurring nightmare that keeps drawing him into the past. It was an original concept, I'll give it that.

Despite Richard's objections, we shot a "happy ending." Our last scene has Al and Ellen reunited, walking off hand in hand down a crowded New York street.

The expectation of happy endings color one's perception of a film, and this psychology applies to life in general. Two Israeli social scientists who received a Nobel Prize for their work on human behavior did a study of people's memories of vacations they had taken. As I remember it, if it rained the first four days and the sun came out on the last three, they had a great vacation. If the reverse occurred and the first four days were sunny and the last three were rainy, their vacation was ruined. It's as simple as that.

I hate to think of the number of films that had their endings reshot so that the audience could leave the theater on a high note. While it might be good for comedies and maybe thrillers, it would turn tragedies into melodramas. It's the tail wagging the dog.

After what can amount to years in development, months in preproduction, weeks of shooting, and five to six months of post-production, the team arrives at the final test: screening the film for an audience. This test screening is complete with cards for the audience to fill out, and focus groups are chosen from the audience to discuss the film. Often, the first question the interviewer asks is

"Who liked the film?" If 70 to 80 percent of the group don't raise their hands, you're in trouble.

The filmmaker is a passive observer. I remember standing in the lobby of the theater where the test screening of *Sea of Love* had taken place. The audience was long gone, the people running the test screening were inside the theater tabulating the results, and I was very much alone. A lot was riding on these results. If the scores were not through the roof, we'd be asked what should be done to help get them there. For me, the screening had already served its purpose. I didn't need the cards.

For the studio, these responses predicted how the film would fare. They were the be-all and end-all. They were hard facts that would color the studio's view of the film. It was that simple. God knows how many films were gutted when the cards took over.

I was waiting on the results when Tom Pollock, the president of the studio, came over and introduced his CEO Sidney Sheinberg. Tom told me that Sid had some interesting ideas for the film, and he'd suggested that Sid share his ideas with the director. Sid proceeded to do just that. He suggested that I drop the dialogue in the last scene where Al and Ellen reunite and replace it with a song. I'd been around long enough by then to know that I couldn't dismiss it out of hand, so instead I feigned interest and told him to let me think about it.

Once you've finished the film, you have to try to protect it.

CHAPTER 23
NIGHT RIDE DOWN

I met Sherry Lansing when I was shooting *Taps* at the Valley Forge Military Academy. She was the president of 20th Century Fox, which was producing the film, and a great friend of Stanley Jaffe, my producer. In fact, they later set up their own production company.

In subsequent meetings with Sherry over the years, I'd always thought our first meeting was when she visited us on the set of *Taps*, but she reminded me that we had actually met when we screened *The Onion Field* for Dan Melnick years before.

Now president of Paramount Pictures, Sherry offered me a thriller, *Night Ride Down*, set against the background of the Pullman porters' strike in the '30s with Harrison Ford attached.

Harrison was in LA for the day and was taking his son to the LA Zoo. The studio thought it would be a good opportunity for us to meet and discuss the project. There we were, talking about the script while his son was visiting with the animals. The meeting had gone well—we scheduled a follow-up at Harrison's home in Jackson Hole.

I hired Darryl Ponicsan to rewrite the script, and we flew up to Jackson Hole to meet with Harrison. The studio had a charter fly us up there. The flight was delayed, and Darryl and I drank gallons of coffee while waiting to take off. It was a small jet used for short hops, and it didn't have a bathroom. The two hour flight felt like eternity.

We spent a couple of days with Harrison in his "garage," which was enormous and included his office. It also housed a large collection of his bikes and cars.

I had the good fortune of hiring Ken Adam as my production designer. He was old school, and his resumé included Stanley Kubrick's *Barry Lyndon* (1975) and *Dr. Strangelove* (1964), as well as the James Bond classics. Ken's research team alone (we were doing a period movie) was larger than the design departments of all my previous films put together. They had actually found the vintage fabrics that the Pullman Company had upholstered their railroad cars in.

I spent days with my cinematographer, Stephen Goldblatt, scouting the Chicago railroad yards—and Chicago has miles and miles of them. I had the wind to my back. We were at full throttle.

Then the rug was pulled out from under us. Harrison jumped ship.

In the middle of our prep, Paramount pulled the plug. They had a very successful franchise in Tom Clancy's *Jack Ryan* series. It was money in the bank, and Harrison was perfect for it. Harrison called with a half-hearted apology. Some lame excuse about our script still needing work.

In a day, a year of work disappeared—literally. Tents were folded, and everyone was off to their next job. You pick yourself up and get on with it. Nothing personal, it's just business.

And don't burn your bridges behind you, you might be lucky enough to work with the very same people next year.

About seven or eight years later, Sherry offered me another film, *Domestic Disturbance*. Again, we had a major star: John Travolta.

CHAPTER 24
DOMESTIC DISTURBANCE (2001)

Domestic Disturbance is the story of a twelve-year-old boy who inadvertently witnesses a murder. The perpetrator is his stepfather, played by Vince Vaughn. Because of the adversarial relationship he has with his stepdad, no one believes the boy. He is the only witness, and his life is in danger. He seeks the protection of his father, played by John Travolta, and the story pivots from a domestic drama about a broken family into a terrifying thriller.

We had a good script, a good cast giving good performances, especially the talented young actor, Matthew O'Leary, as well as Vince Vaughn as the killer hiding in plain sight and Steve Buscemi as an unwelcome visitor from the past. Yes, we had seen it all before, but that didn't dampen my enthusiasm. One of my favorite thrillers was Hitchcock's *Shadow of a Doubt* (1943), in which a beloved uncle is the killer.

We set our drama in Wilmington, North Carolina, a coastal city with a small town feel. Much like the northwestern town in *Shadow of a Doubt*, it added a peaceful innocence that belied what lay beneath.

When John Travolta was working, he set the pace. The call sheet might indicate an eight a.m. start, but John's working habits included a lavish breakfast in his trailer.

One morning, frustrated by the late start, which put pressure on us to get the day's work done on time, I visited John as he was having his breakfast. It was a feast fit for a king, from eggs Benedict to beef Wellington, with silver and linen to match. I guess years of stardom had earned him that. Ever his affable self, John invited me to join him, assuring me that if we didn't finish the work today, there was always tomorrow. Of course, the studio didn't quite see it that way. But they didn't share their concerns with John, they shared them with me. I love John, he just had other priorities.

Not all of the drama on set ends up in the film. Sometimes it's between takes, so to speak. Sometime in the after-hours, Vince Vaughn and Steve Buscemi were at a bar filled with townies. Actors are lightning rods, drawing both the adoration and resentment of the locals, especially when women and liquor are involved. Words were exchanged, and a brawl had spilled out into the street where Steve, when challenged, didn't back down. Steve was tough. He had been a New York fireman before finding his calling. The townie pulled out a knife and slashed Steve's throat, missing his jugular by mere millimeters.

I slept soundly through it all. Unlike Steve and Vince, I had an early call, which kept me out of late-night dramas. Fortunately, after a few weeks, Steve was able to rejoin us.

On the last day of our shoot, the unthinkable occurred. Planes crashed into the World Trade Center buildings and the Pentagon. 9/11 overshadowed everything. John called to tell me he was flying to New York to lend his support. He had his own plane and asked me to join him. We landed at a small airport in White Plains—all the major airports had been shut down—and were escorted to the outskirts Ground Zero by boat. We visited the makeshift memorial to the firemen who had given their lives to save others. It was the closest we could get to the graveyard of what had once been the Twin Towers. For years, I had seen them every day from the terrace of my apartment on lower Fifth.

After a few a days in a city dark with the trauma of 9/11, I returned to LA. The editing rooms at Paramount became my home.

My final edit of *Domestic Disturbance* came in at an hour and fifty-five minutes. After endless test screenings, we were down to an hour and fifteen minutes. We even rewrote and reshot the final scene to get that extra boost—to have the audience out of their seats cheering. It had worked for *Fatal Attraction* (1987), which Sherry and Stanley Jaffe had produced. I had seen it with the original ending, which was dark, and then I had seen it with the new ending, which had the audience cheering. The film grossed over two hundred million dollars, enough to make anyone a believer.

In spite of my misgivings, the test screening scores had definitely improved, and the studio was predicting a strong opening weekend.

We opened against *Monsters, Inc.* (2001), a children's film that had a built-in audience and was sure to dominate the box office that weekend. When I pointed this out, I was assured that *Monsters* was for a different audience. I was told Travolta's sweet spot were women in their forties and fifties, fans of *Saturday Night Fever* (1977) and *Grease* (1978). Sadly, many of those forty- and fifty-year-olds were taking their kids and grandkids to see *Monsters, Inc.*

CHAPTER 25
ODDS AND ENDS

Al Pacino called after seeing *Middle of the Night* by Paddy Chayefsky, the great screenwriter who had written gems like *Network* (1976) and *Marty* (1955).

Made in 1959, it stars Fredric March as Jerry Kingsley, an older businessman who has fallen in love with his secretary, played by Kim Novak. After seeing the film and reading Chayefsky's screenplay, I was on board. I thought Al would be perfect for March. Though in his early seventies, he had an energy and a youthfulness. He could easily play an older man who was still filled with the vitality that would make a relationship with a younger woman believable.

After a table reading of Chayefsky's screenplay, we realized we needed a rewrite. We'd envisioned a small intimate film, basically a two-character piece. *Brief Encounter* (1945), David Lean's masterpiece, came to mind.

We also needed financing.

We met Ed Walson at a dinner party. Money was his calling card. I remember him arriving in a chauffeur-driven vintage Rolls-Royce. Ed loved movie stars. That's why he was there. He may not have been the richest person in the world, but he did have his own Gulfstream. A regional cable business might make you rich, but it certainly won't make you famous. Being in the company of movie stars can raise your game.

Ed had already had a bite of the apple. He had financed some of Woody Allen's recent films. He had enjoyed Woody's company but was dumped when Woody moved to Amazon. *Middle of the Night* came along at the right time for each of us.

With financing in place, we brought in David Mamet to do the rewrite. Both Al and I had a relationship with David, Al's going all the way back to *American Buffalo*. David had written an adaptation of *Dr. Jekyll and Mr. Hyde* for Al and me that fell by the wayside. And there we were, together again.

Middle of the Night was right in his wheelhouse. He turned it into a noir-ish drama in which nothing was what it appeared to be. Al and I loved it, but it wasn't clear sailing. Al had commitments that kept him busy for the upcoming year, and time began to take its toll.

In trying to find a major talent to play the younger woman, we were running into strong headwinds. The #MeToo movement had swept in, and our script couldn't make it past the stars' agents who closed the book after reading "older man, younger woman."

An underlying friction with Ed also began to manifest. He began to think of himself as a real producer. The money began to assert itself. The tail began to wag the dog. I don't know what external forces were involved, but it was obviously about money. It's always about the money. Ed demanded that our rock-bottom budget had to be reduced even further. It was as though the budget we had arrived at was plucked out of the air. Hopefully, he wasn't maintaining his airplane on that principle—he'd have been arguing with the pilots about how much fuel was needed to get to the destination. Who knows, he might have thought he could actually fly the airplane. And then it was over.

Ed was out. Al and I moved on.

There's always the next one. Sometimes it's a book you can't put down, even if it has a title that screams exploitation. Joyce Carol Oates's novel *Rape: A Love Story* is the story of a brutal rape and the love of a daughter and a cop who avenge it. The book's jacket copy sets the tone:

> Teena Maguire should not have tried to shortcut her way home that Fourth of July. Not after midnight, not through Rocky Point Park. Not the way she was dressed: tank top, denim cutoffs, high-heeled sandals. Not with her twelve-year-old daughter, Bethie. Not with packs of local guys running loose on hormones, rage, and alcohol. A victim of gang rape, left for dead in the park

> boathouse, the once vital and sexy Teena Maguire can now only regret that she has survived.

For me, it was a film begging to be made. Too raw for the studios, I took the indie road. The script by John Mankiewicz, which stayed true to Oates's novel, was unrelenting in invoking the drama that begins in that boathouse.

Script in hand, I made the rounds of the established indies. They rejected it, saying it was a vigilante movie. Well, so was *Unforgiven* (1992), Clint Eastwood's masterpiece that opens with a brutal rape, or, for that matter, John Ford's epic *The Searchers* (1956). It was to no avail, and we were in the hands of the bottom feeders who didn't even read the scripts. They just wanted to know who's in it, who they could sell to the foreign market, and what their cut would be compared to the budget of the film. The only one I could raise money on was the hero of the film, the cop who becomes Teena Maguire's avenging angel.

Samuel L. Jackson—who I had met on *Sea of Love*, where he had a short but brilliant moment—was perfect for the part, but the foreign market just wasn't there. I thought maybe if I could find an actress who could pull her weight to play Teena, but that didn't happen. The rape scene was a nonstarter for many actresses.

I finally was able to cast Nicolas Cage, an actor who still had some weight in the foreign market. Unfortunately, between his salary, which came off the top, and the bottom feeders' cut, there wasn't enough money to shoot in Niagara Falls, the novel's setting that plays an important role in the story's unfolding. I found myself scouting locations in Atlanta, which fit our budget but had nothing to do with our story.

My belief in *Rape: A Love Story* blinded me to reality, and there I was in Atlanta, trying to make believe it was Niagara Falls.

The final straw was spending that week in Atlanta with a hack producer before coming to my senses and taking the next plane out.

I'd suggested that Nic and I put part of our fees in the production so we could at least have some of the money we needed, and his agent firmly replied, "Not a dime."

My ambition to make films on my own terms gave way to the financial realities. Whether it was shooting a film in Bulgaria that took place in Washington, DC, because it was cheaper there or finding a rich financier (too good to be true) whose only ambition was to be in the company of movie stars, I simply wasn't able to strip away everything I stood for just to get a film made.

EPILOGUE

Seeing *City Hall* again recently was like a reunion. I was in the company of all those talented players, most of them no longer with us, brought together by Bo Goldman's brilliant screenplay. Al Pacino as the mayor of New York, carrying the weight of that office, and in perfect step, John Cusack, his protégé and his conscience. I'd forgotten how good John was. The final scene between Al and John, so full of regrets of what could have been. All of my major players—Danny Aiello as the larger-than-life politician, Tony Franciosa as the menacing mafioso, Martin Landau as the all-too-fallible judge—had a lifetime of distinguished work behind them. And, of course, Al Pacino, John Cusack, and Bridget Fonda. How lucky I was to have brought them together in the service of a screenplay that was worthy of their talents. So many of them are gone now, *City Hall* a part of their legacy.

Not to mention the brilliant cinematography of my dear friend, Michael Seresin. We had started together on our first film over thirty years earlier. And Jerry Goldsmith's melancholy score, so rich in emotion, completed our symphony.

City Hall fulfilled a dream that had started when I walked into Jerry Plucer's studio. I didn't know it then, and I didn't know it when Joe Wambaugh took a chance on me or when Stanley Jaffe did. As John Cusack says at the end of *City Hall*, "You have to be lucky."

It's been an interesting journey with its share of speed bumps. What has stood by me through it all has been my first love, photography. From an eleven-by-fourteen studio camera to a 35mm Nikon S to a Leica Monochrom, I have never stopped catching the light.

ACKNOWLEDGMENTS

To Arthur Chang, whose assistance was invaluable and to Jacob Hoye, my editor, whose welcoming words, "It's a lovely read," invited me in, thank you.

My thanks to John Burnham, Rick Carlivati, and all the others who are in this memoir or should be!

PHOTO CREDITS

Pages 86 & 177—Album/Alamy
Page 87—A7A Collection/Alamy
Pages 102 & 128—AJ Pics/Alamy
Page 104—Maximum Film/Alamy
Pages 112, 114 & 165 —IFA Film/Alamy
Page 123—RGR Collection/Alamy
Page 142—Impress/Alamy
Page 163—Cinematic Collection/Alamy
Page 167—Universal Pictures/Alamy

All other photographs are courtesy of Harold Becker.